KU-661-472

Angel Journey

For all the angels on this journey, who had human faces.
For Albie, Finn and Rory and the messages they bring.

Angel Journey

Suzanne Power

LONDUBH BOOKS

First published in 2010 by

Londubh Books

18 Casimir Avenue, Harold's Cross, Dublin 6w, Ireland

www.londubh.ie

1 3 5 4 2

Origination by Londubh Books; cover by redrattledesign

Printed in Ireland by ColourBooks, Baldoyle Industrial Estate, Dublin 13

ISBN: 978-1-907535-14-7

CONTENTS

Introduction: That Has Made All the Difference

In a cold snap, close to spring but still winter, I went to meet a publisher, in a place of her choice. It was no more than a hundred metres from the room in which I decided to live a better life, with the help of a psychotherapist, who, many years after I left therapy, became my friend.

My friend had moved away to England. The day of the meeting I had a call from her and said where I was going. 'That's very strange,' she answered. 'I'm here visiting too. I'll see you when your meeting is over.'

She arrived and the publisher was still there. The publisher left. My friend asked me what the meeting had been about.

'A book on angels.' I was quiet.

'Ah.' My friend has heard all the world's stories. 'Will you do it?'

'Yes,' I answered. 'Not straight away.'

'Why?'

'I'm scared. I don't know what I think about angels.'

'But you have faith. What does your faith sense say?'

'I'll get over the fear.' The months of mental wrangling ahead were already casting shadows in front of me.

We walked around the corner to look at the house she had left behind and I had left behind. We met our past and then we got into our cars and went back to our futures. It occurred to me that neither of us had ever anticipated meeting each other again, outside therapy, or ending up where we did. We were examples that you have no control, only destiny to follow. And, for my friend and me, only spirit to guide you.

The story of our friendship is the story of this book. Journey books are a problem and a wonder. They bring both fear and desire. The fear is: how long will the journey take? The desire is not to know, but to experience. Journey books are about letting doors open, rather than anticipating and deciding where the doors are. Much like following what it says in the guidebook when you visit a foreign country, a planned journey is going to be shorter and will run more smoothly but there is an underlying unease, a sense of being cheated: someone has been there before you, eaten that meal, slept in that bed. You are emulating rather than experiencing.

Or you can just turn up in the country and talk to the people you meet and see where that takes you. That is the kind of road Robert Frost's poem refers to. That is the road less travelled.

And taking it does make all the difference.

One road can be obeyed; the other involves risk and meeting the uncertain self in uncertain times. When we all hope spiritual guidance will bring us greater certainties, instead it brings us more of the same, only worse, because there is no last place, no last refuge. Only the open days and eternal nights when your fear says, 'Turn back.'

Unplanned journeys break all the principles of safety and of guidance. They go out of control. But they are part of a more vibrant scheme that is incarnation rather than laboratory experiment. The experiences are new, the territory fresh and ungoverned. Denying my training, not setting interviews up but letting conversations happen and going to the next place these conversations led me, whether it was Donegal on a storm day or my neighbour down the road, I discovered a treasure I never knew existed. This was how I met my angels, or how they met me.

The book did not rest.

The stories I heard were incredible but not outlandish, not lost in magic.

Eighteen months later. It's a book about angels. But it's not about crystals, wings, it's not spirit-lite, it's not chants and gilt. It's a real book about light and dark. It's a book about personal journeys and nervous breakdowns, about catastrophe and rebuild, it's about the messages from spirit that get us through reality. It's about the evil we have to overcome and release ourselves from. It is horror and honour. It is tragedy and the triumphs to be had even as we go through it. It's not about cards, or divination. It's about divine moments.

It's about messages, or, as Donagh, a priest, potter and philosopher, whom you meet in the last chapter, calls them: 'God's thoughts.' And also: 'The narrow bases we build futures on.'

'Reality in my experience is usually odd. It is not neat, not obvious, not what you expect…Reality, in fact, is usually something you could not have guessed,' C.S. Lewis wrote, shortly after his conversion from atheism to theism.

I had no idea reality could be so perfect in its turmoil and so much like what Nietzsche described: 'Out of chaos comes a dancing star.'

The main fight was between fear and knowing. Our instincts, which are informed by intuition, not by conscious mind, are capable of reaching the truth our intellect often prevents. It took me a long time to get past the fear but the book wouldn't go away or rest. One of the reasons I knew it would take a while to write was the amount of truth it would require from me. I am lonely in my desire to answer the call of my life unconditionally. I could not deal in half measures on this subject. Pablo Neruda, a statesman and venerated poet, picked up stray dogs in his loneliness. I've done that. I am a stray dog. I walk alone but I am helped in my aloneness by what I know as God. And there are messages from that source and the deliverers of messages have been called angels throughout centuries, throughout persuasions. As a postman's daughter I have a great respect for delivery services of any kind.

One of the first signposts for the journey was in reading the literature. I read about how much angels cross the faith experience. They are true intermediaries in not belonging to any one catechism. So this book embraces all the God ways and paths. All the truths and all the versions of spirit, from shamanism to strict orthodoxy. I have been led only by the conversations and not to conclusion. I spoke to those who still believe in organised religion and those who do not.

I spoke to those who don't believe in anything at all. My decision was to make no decisions, since every decision is a judgement. If the phone rang and it was someone whose views I didn't subscribe to, I still went to meet them. I follow the definition of being liberal which says you must respect opinions you don't hold yourself.

This took me out of my comfort zone. I learned true listening. Anyone who features in the pages is someone I believed to be authentic, grounded and capable. Anyone featured was allowed to express the entirety of their views to me and any editing of these views was done purely for reasons of space. Each interview could have been a chapter and I spoke to hundreds of people. Every person was made to understand that I would talk to anyone and that the next anyone might not be their version of angelic.

The stories featured are all of people who had stories beyond themselves, who stretched their humanity to find their way, who had experienced occurrences that could not be explained by logic but held a meaning they couldn't forget. They all told the truth about their choice of God and their miracles.

This is the true account of my angelic journey and it pays no mind to those who think real life can be solved by wands, who retreat into magic at the expense of reality. We are all going uphill: how much help we get is dependent on how open we are in our struggle. One woman who was literally barricaded in her own home, who was mentally ill after years of abuse, says, 'When I was in the horror I prayed I would learn what I needed to learn and that the purpose be met. I knew God was with me, from the messages I received.'

What does an angel journey comprise?

The word 'angel' has a journey as varied and global as the phenomenon. It is a fusion of the Old English and Old French, a derivative of Latin, with roots in Greek – *angelos* – but the original seed is Hebrew: *mal'akh*. All its transmutations, all its flights through philosophies and ages have brought the same meaning – angels are messengers. Messengers of God.

An angel journey, then, is a journey to source. It is a belief that your version of God is giving you messages, to persuade you somewhere inside you that there is a soul and a purpose, a determination that wants to join with a universal energy beyond bones, blood and heart.

People are turning increasingly to more individualised interpretations of what it means to believe and what to believe in. I found myself on more than one occasion wondering if what I was being told was out of need rather than an insight. But all insight comes out of need. An angel journey is a walk towards, a walk with, the unseen. What is imagined or felt to be close to God and not of ourselves, although across religions angels are known to take human form and dwell among us. My interpretation is: if we are human we can be angels too.

The months spent with this book involved the answer of doubts. I didn't get the angel phenomenon, still don't in its most structured form. The last thing a refugee from hierarchical religion needs is another hierarchy. But I can see why this appeals. And I decided from the first meeting on my journey not to judge what was said or negate it in any shape or form. There are people who believe in what I cannot believe in. We are different strings on the same instrument, all capable of harmonising if allowed our individuality.

Most angel books are written by those who have experienced epiphany and are moved to write about it. I am not such a person. I am not distinct in anything that has happened to me. I am distinct only in my ability to listen to the stories I hear and to remain open to them. I have never seen an angel. I have never felt wings.

But I've had messages. Things that have happened that are inexplicable. My faith is not strong enough nor my pragmatism weak enough for me to consider myself prophetic or profound. I am you. I am going about my daily life struggling and occasionally I get a message from a source that is neither inside me nor around me. These occasions have happened rarely and before now I examined my heart and mind before sharing them with anyone other than close friends.

I have spoken to some people who are the same as me, who have been given more powerful insights and experiences than mine, who have come from dark places and times: who have murdered, lost babies, been betrayed and had their families violated but have been given something outside their humanity and their capability, to get through and become more.

In my prevarications I had two key conversations. One was with Mary T., a feminist theologian and an historian. She has lectured and pondered and studied and debated her subject for more than four decades. She has written a three-volume series called *Women and Christianity*. When I called her to say what I was doing her instant response was: 'Good. This is good. Time for something real to be written in this area. You're journeying; you're not an expert.'

I laughed and said, 'Angels for beginners.'

'You're not going to get into the quick solution or the mumbo-jumbo when you write this. You're not about statues and card readings, you're about the real thing,' another friend Maeve, who has worked in theology and academia all her life, tackled me when I lost faith. 'If it's human, you'll write about your anxiety in revealing yourself.'

Mary T. also writes about apprehension and wonderment. My angelic journey and those of others was a mixture of the two. At every moment of apprehension, I was given wonder to get me going again. That has made all the difference.

I didn't know at the time that I was accepting a journey back to acceptance. I have been writing for a living for a long time but I had stopped writing for my soul for the past five years. In those five years I wrote only one piece about what I was truly going through.

I have brought people on in their creativity because I understand the cage it is housed in. My students and colleagues had no idea, because I sounded so free, that I was in the same cage.

I had no idea at the start that by the end I would have realised, fully, that there are angels. But not in the place you'd expect them to be. I didn't know the angel journey was taking me back to the person I had discarded in order to meet the genuine conditions of my life. Provision for children, coping with tragedy, dealing with separation and chronic illness – these have been strong features of the past decade. It's a decade in which I lost myself and found another, better me, waiting in the dark room.

All along this road less travelled there have been signposts. They have made all the difference. When I had my last conversation for this book, it was in the wildflower meadow at the back of my house with the woman with whom I had my first conversation.

'Bernadette,' I said, 'Thanks for the gift of your story.' The wildflower meadow took two summers to come on. We planted it on soil that had been landscaped by someone we knew was either a visionary or a madman.

This year, for the first time, it has flourished. It took seasons of belief and waiting, which is an action.

Like all ends, you begin at the end. So here is the end of my story, right at the start. Here is the journey that took it all out of me and put it all back.

Note
Some of the contributors to *Angel Journey* have changed their names in order to remain anonymous. While all the stories were told to the author she has had to abridge them. Every care has been taken with this and any errors in the accounts are her own and not those of the contributors.

1

EXPECTING TO FLY

There you stood on the edge of your feather. Expecting to fly.
                                                            Neil Young

It's important, to show I am open to those who have shared their stories with me, that I share some of my own. I have no truck with wings but I am moved by things and urges beyond my understanding. I know the messages that come, the messengers that provide them, are to be listened to with respect.

The first story here occurred a couple of years ago and I wrote about it in my newspaper column, because it seemed churlish not to. The economic downturn had started and I experienced a good fortune. A Christmas miracle.

In 2007 I stood in a field and asked if I should build a house. The answer was firm and yes. The economy, my circumstances, the state of my relationship, nothing agreed. But I wanted my children to go to a school they would look back on happily and my partner and I decided to do something we never do. Gamble. We put them into school miles away from our house. We built a house with a view to selling our own when the time came to move. And we did sell it. Almost. But the buyers pulled out within days of signing, having already spent significant sums on surveys and the like.

We got the phone call while we were choosing things for the new house. We put everything back and cancelled all the orders we had placed, losing deposits on carpets, wooden flooring, stoves and white goods.

'I know it's going to be okay,' I said to my partner.

'You tell me how.'

I knew we were in trouble because he is the optimist.

The following day we put an advertisement in the local paper and a man rented the old property. I knew he was the right person, for some reason the rational would explain as mad, even though I had never met him, because he had gone to the same tiny school in the middle of nowhere my children now attend. I see this as making energetic sense rather than commonsense. As the Dalai Lama says: 'I am open to the guidance of synchronicity, and do not let expectations hinder my path.'

In plain Irish English, what appears to be lunacy is often the right thing to do.

This solved a part of our problem. But we had no money to buy white goods now that we were not selling the old home.

I was owed $1500 dollars in tax withheld erroneously by an American publisher for four years. I had given up on it when told that the American revenue system – the IRS – does not accept claims over three years old. I had dealt with their offices in London, New York, Philadelphia and Austin, Texas, over those three years.

But the night the house sale collapsed, I had a stroke of inspiration or desperation: 'Let's be positive. Let's say, for the next half-hour, we'll give this one more shot. In the next thirty minutes we'll try to earn $1500 dollars.'

My partner agreed and went to make the phone calls since I would end up in the nuthouse talking to them. I stood in the kitchen clearing dinner and putting out washing on the clothes horse, whispering under my breath, 'We will get it.' He was still on the phone when I put the kids to bed. He was still on the phone when I came out of the shower. When he came through to the bedroom it was close to midnight and he said a Ms Devine of the IRS would like to speak to me.

I took the name as my cue and agreed. And she was officious, then not officious, then laughed and then was considerate. I told her I was a gobshite who needed a fridge and a washing machine. She didn't understand gobshite.

'There is no record of you on our system, Ma'am. The claim's outside the time limit allowed, by over a year. But I would like you to

write a letter to the following and send it to the following and I want
to tell you now, if I could write cheques, I would, in your case. But I
don't think you have a hope of getting it.'

'Thanks, Ms Devine,' I said. 'A bit of angel dust your way.' I don't
know why I said that, it just seemed the right thing to say at the time.

'I could use it, Ma'am. Now if you have no further questions, good
night.'

'Happy Christmas.'

'Happy Christmas to you too.'

Even if we managed to get the form, the claim was well outside
the three-year limit for filing. We laughed and made some joke about
selling the engagement ring. I don't have one. I wrote one more letter
and faxed it to the person Ms Devine told me about.

My spirituality is more pragmatic than little gilted porcelain
figures with net wings. To me it's like the country and western end
of spirituality. So I don't know what made me say that to a woman
on the other side of the Atlantic, in the middle of another continent.
I went for a walk the next day. The postman came while I was in the
loo and I didn't like going to the post. It was full of bills.

There was only one letter.

From the American Embassy in Ballsbridge.

Inside a cheque from the United States Treasury.

For the full amount.

I'm looking at it. Right now. There's a statue of Liberty printed on
the cheque. Now unless Ms Devine used a space shuttle, she didn't
have a hand in it. I don't know who did. I photocopied it and stuck it
on my filing cabinet with the word 'Trust' above it. $1500, or €1200,
gets you all you need in fridges, cookers and washing machines.
$1500, the week after your house sale falls through, when you can't
afford two mortgages and you're facing repossession within months,
losing every foothold you ever had on the financial ladder, makes for
trusting in something beyond.

When I wrote the column, I wrote this line: 'I'm going to start
believing in miracles again. They've happened to me more than once.
I just forgot.' I sent the piece to Ms Devine.

There is more than one story in my life like this. More than once I backed away from this book because if you can't be honest you shouldn't write books. You can't sit in front of other people and extract their stories on belief and believing, without giving yourself over for scrutiny, without letting cynics pick your bones. I am so afraid to write what's coming next. But the voice I listen to, of my instinct, I believe is the voice of spirit.

I don't go to church, I talk to the higher power and I shout a good bit. I know there's a god because I am often so angry at her. Then, in collating the stories of others, I collated my own. I have never expected to fly but I have always flown. I have expected to fly, then never let myself. I am more than one person and the professional in me knows what journalists do with these kinds of statements. Mitch Albom, ex-sportswriter, used the boxing ring to warn me about this: 'When you come out of the sceptic corner and say you believe in something, the commentary changes. Remember if they're cynical, they're writing about themselves.'

What happened to me over the cheque happened to me more than once. I just forgot. Here are some of the stories, some of the messages I forgot:

When I was a small girl I used to play with my imaginary twins. My paternal grandmother was a twin. Uncle and she lived in the same house for most of their lives. My grandfather never got as close to her as her brother did. My parents presumed my twins were my Nanny and Uncle. My twins were boys.

At about eight years old I stopped playing with them but I remember thinking throughout my teens that if I was a mother I would be a mother of twins. Then I went into my twenties, married, and my first husband and I travelled a lot. I struggled to think of bringing children into a world I was not sure I could even manage.

I lived by the sea in Skerries, in a house where, as one friend put it, when you opened the door there was 'nothing but weather'. The way the light played on the water convinced me. We moved in as autumn came and skies clouded over. Within a week of our unpacking, the wind was throwing seawater on to the windows. I loved the wildness, the possibilities, in every storm. The fact that I was beside a fire watching nature perform outside.

As soon as the world calmed I was off beachcombing, picking up lobster pots and rope lengths for decorating the garden one day. Collecting storm-shaped stones and pieces of coloured glass to put in a jar that sat in the window of my study.

I ran along the road to Ardgillan, I ran the South Strand, scrambled along the coastal rocks to a Martello tower near Loughshinny and couldn't believe my luck that I was only forty minutes from Dublin and work. It didn't seem possible. But there were days, staring at the tail lights of another trapped vehicle in a jam that added an hour to the journey, that I wished I could just work and look at my sea view.

Be careful what you wish for.

After a trip to Peru, I got a January virus, combined with travel vaccination after-effects. No matter how hard I tried, I couldn't get back to running. I had just done a strenuous hike in the Andes and I couldn't get round the Skerries headland.

In February I decided I was being lazy and stupid and should walk in to see my doctor for a tonic. A distance of half a mile. I made it as far as a rock on the North Strand and sat, looking at the tide seeping out, leaving the sand glistening, and fighting the need to close my eyes. I knew something was very wrong.

Two months later I had resigned from my job as features editor of a Sunday newspaper. I had a clinical diagnosis of post-viral or chronic fatigue syndrome, also known as ME.

The result was I got to see my sea view, every hour of every day, for over a year. I barely left the bedroom and when I did it was only to lie down somewhere else. I spent a year being unable to run away from myself, being held by a mystery that sapped my energy and left me bedridden.

I was obsolete. I was a former athlete, former editor, former presenter, former party girl, former adventurer, former every-thing.

I was nothing.

When you are bedridden it doesn't just help to have a sea view.

It restores you.

I watched the heron fish the rock pools outside my window and I learned that waiting is an action, as is resting. A phone call to the ME helpline and I happened to speak to Eric, a retired journalist, who got through to me: 'You'll still be able to write, it'll just have to be a different kind. Write the book you always wanted to.'

My husband, when he heard this, went straight to a shop and bought me a laptop. At the time laptops were expensive and we had just lost my income. It remains the best thing that anyone has ever done for me.

It took me days of rest to get a few hours' work done. I no longer ran or even walked on the beaches. But I watched other people and became accepting of the fact that this was my time for observation, not participation. I have always been active and it's a trait of my personality that I avoid things through activity. I couldn't ignore the voice calling me to write fiction any more.

On the days I felt I couldn't do it, I just merged with the seascape and became part of the cloud changes, the sky's difference. I let myself drift on the open waves and imagine.

When I finished the book, two years later, it went to a UK publishing house that took a further two years to publish it. By that time I had recovered, with the help of the heron.

An editor, who was responsible for thinking of jackets, said, 'I feel a heron on an Irish shoreline is the right kind of cover.' The heron is mentioned only once in the story. She had no knowledge of the assistance I had been given, in illness, watching a bird practised in stillness, using it to feed himself.

While I was sick, my neighbour at the time was a woman who had a psychic gift. She did healings on me, she listened to me when I said I wished I was dead, and she told me I would not only get better, I had two children waiting to come to me. Her message: 'They're close, but you're not ready. They'll come when you call.' Something crossed her face and I knew she saw more than *when* I was ready, but *who* I would be ready with. I put it down to a disagreement she had with my husband, a man you couldn't disagree with he's so amiable. I thought she hadn't quite forgiven him. 'You are being helped by an older woman and she's writing "Two and two is four" on a blackboard and laughing. She's in an old schoolhouse by a stream.'

My husband had nursed me, fed me, loved me and kept me sane

with his humour. We had become separated. His body was well and mine was still. He went sailing and my eyes were blind to what I was seeing, a man I loved but whose life and interests I couldn't share. I didn't know what to say. I went with the first thing that came to me in a monastery, where I was on retreat. There I made another lifelong friend: a monk who specialised in answering the condition of souls that don't fit in churches but belong somewhere and can no longer find their place. I said to him, 'I'm lonely in my marriage.' He told me everything worth something brings loneliness with it.

I felt relief: no decision that turned mine and his life upside down to be made then. Just accept this as another stage in a lifelong relationship. Another rite of passage. I went home and was well enough to accept commissions. One of them was to interview the actress Pauline Collins. She was an Oscar nominee for *Shirley Valentine*, filmed in Greece, and not as forthcoming as that screen character, but at one stage in a hard interview, she said: 'You need to do a Vision Quest.'

Pauline gave me the number of a former polar explorer, Sir Wally Herbert and his wife, Dame Marie Herbert. They lived in Kingussie in the Scottish Highlands. I found out, only when I arrived, that Vision Quest involved going out into wilderness for thirty-six hours with no food and some water, with nothing to occupy you but weather and landscape. You were not allowed to walk: you had to sit in a stone circle of your creation and wait for your message to come. The quest involved a night alone.

No vision came of my husband and me and the baby. But that week was one of the most moving and spiritual experiences of my life. I left the Highlands elated and worried. The week had brought me home to myself after the long illness, and frightening aspects of my recovery were rising. I still couldn't accept that I was married to a man who hadn't the same path or interests.

The same night that I sat in the stone circle of my creation, waiting for my vision to present itself, five hundred miles away a man sat in an East End pub trying to enjoy his birthday drinks, wishing he could meet someone to have a child with, feeling more alone in his four decades than he had ever felt and closer to not being with someone he could share his life with than he had ever felt.

He was to become the father of my children.

I couldn't settle when I came home. My heart raced every time I tried to sit still. A month after Scotland, I was in Greece, on my own, visiting the monasteries of Meteora, built into cliff faces, monks raised and lowered in wicker baskets on pulley systems. No expecting to fly there. Over forty degrees: the lightest of clothing feels like a sable coat. You cannot move and the only thing that does is your sweat. But I was walking from one monastery to another, using up health earned over two years of stillness, needing to talk to monks and finding no answers.

I left for Athens because I couldn't bear to be in a place of pilgrimage with no alleviation for my desolation. The journey back was hotter than any version of hell you care to conjure. I kept a close eye on the signs for proximity to Athens. Like when I was a child in my father's car on a long journey: 'How many more miles now?' I asked so many times he clouded the windscreen and wrote the figure on it. My eyes glazed with the need to be free of the bus, the sweated cloister. I kept a close eye on the signs. Each one. I saw a sign for a monastery. Having just spent a week walking to several, in heat and dust, I thought it was the last thing I would need: we were only forty kilometres from Athens and the Plaka and the best vegetarian food I have ever put in my mouth. But I got off the bus at the side of the highway and walked back to the sign.

Then, looking left and right to make sure there was no traffic, I kicked it hard for a few minutes, then sat under it. And wept.

The monastery of Hosios Loukas, or Venerable St Luke, is situated in a scenic site on the slopes of Mount Helicon. If you think scenic and slope, you know it involves a climb. It was founded in the early tenth century by the hermit, whose relics are kept in the monastery to this day. He was famous for having predicted the conquest of Crete.

The main shrine of the monastery is the tomb of St Luke, originally situated in the vault, but later placed at the juncture of the its two churches. The monastery derived its wealth (including funds required for construction) from the fact that the relics of St

Luke were said to have exuded myron, a sort of perfumed oil which produced healing miracles. Pilgrims hoping for miraculous help were encouraged to sleep by the side of the tomb in order to be healed by incubation.

The relics had been moved to more sumptuous surroundings. But the old stone sarcophagus was left in the vault.

There is a gap in my travel journal. It starts at the point where I get to the monastery gates and finishes with me back in Athens, a demented oven, trying to ignore what happened. *I have a paralysis of the soul. After what I felt yesterday at the monastery I can't feel God, I just feel challenge and death.* These are the only lines that refer to what happened. But that's okay. I remember. When I got off the bus I looked at it leave and cried.

The lines before 'paralysis' talk about the journey from the crossroads to the monastery: Why did I get off? I had kilometres to walk with a full pack, in thirty-nine degrees of heat. An old Citroën van pulled up in front of me and a skeleton covered in muscle and skin got out. He was bow-legged and there were only three teeth in his head. He threw open the back door of his van for my pack and walked back to take it from me. I didn't argue. My Greek greeting was ignored; he began speaking in French. He was a Frenchman living in Greece, *après la guerre*. His ignition was without a key and his gear stick was an old walking cane. The dashboard had disappeared and the engine workings were masked by a sheet of metal welded in. He filled my bag with pears, refused my custard cream biscuits, money and a photo opportunity. He drove me beyond Distomo, the town, to the monastery gates. He told me he was an 'ermite'. A hermit, living in the environs and in the shadow of one of Greece's most famous. Living alone and without guile. At the gate, I saw him get out to fill up with a jug of what must have been fuel. I wondered how many kilometres he had gone out of his way, or if he existed. In this small place, he must have been known but no one hailed him on the road, or in the town. When he left I wanted him to come back for me.

This is what I remember. Inside the monastery a coach tour of Americans had arrived to admire the gilding, the relics. I was unable to be near anyone, so I went down into the cool of the crypt. The tour followed me, soon got bored of shade and stone and went up to where the photo opportunities were. I sat for a while, enjoying the sensation of my body temperature dropping, the stillness of the air. I put my hands on the walls and then to my skin. My pack was in the corner furthest from the entrance. When the bus left I was going to sleep down here. A siesta, then head back to Distomo for dinner and a bus. I ate a Pierre pear and wrapped it in the almost transparent toilet roll. Then I stood up, and put my hands on the sarcophagus. Something flashed before my eyes. I said, 'I know.'

Then I left. A young couple, Belgian, were getting into their hire car. I asked if they could drive me to the town. They drove me further, back to the same crossroads. We had a pleasant conversation about travel. They were going to get married when they got back. A honeymoon before the wedding, so they could enjoy their day.

I bought a forty-drachma phone card and told my husband. Forty-drachma phone calls can change lives. When I came home from Greece we began to say goodbye to each other.

The message at Hosias Loukas is for two people to know. My ex-husband and me.

Four months later my husband and I went to see his parents in the home I'd visited for over a decade and explained that we were separating. They were tortured at the prospect. I love those people as much as I love him still. It was harder to leave that man than it was to recover from illness. When they asked why, he said to them, 'Suzanne realises things before the rest of us. She always has.'

He could have called me any number of names for all the care he had put into helping me back to health and all the hurt I was now causing in going. The night before I left we had a meal together and 'Time to Say Goodbye' was playing. He saw the humour in it, as he does in everything. He is the most gracious man in all he does and in all he is. I wasn't smiling. I was someone who knew nothing.

I went back to Greece, I bought the last place on a writing course with Sue Townsend, a woman I had interviewed twice over a ten-year period. She told me to do her course and I did on a whim. On the first night a man sat beside me and introduced himself as Albie. I asked if this was short for anything. He said it wasn't short for anything, or long for anything, it was just Albie. He had decided to do a course at the last minute, instead of going to India, where he was going to work for a while. I knew I was going to love him for the rest of my life. This was not a good feeling because I saw the pain he would bring with him. He was broken and so was I. We have a dear friend who met us both on that holiday. She is a psychotherapist. She said, 'You work on a spiritual level, you work on an emotional level, but on a practical level you are going to have your work cut out!'

A man who lives on the island where we met has the gift of second sight. He offered to read my palm for my birthday but when he took it up he refused. I know why now.

Two years later. I did a shamanic journey, to drums across midnight. We had just begun to try for a baby and given our separate histories we were sure it would take a good time to conceive. I was living in Ireland and he was in London. It was New Year's Eve. I asked if I was going to have a baby. The answer was two children, running fast. I put it down to him and me, learning to grow up together. I asked when the baby would come. I heard, August/September, over and over.

I did a test. It was positive.

Seven weeks later my friend, who met us both in Greece, who told us what work we would have together, came to see me in Dublin. I was pregnant. Her twin boys had just turned twenty-one. We were due to have a celebratory weekend. Two things happened. She got violently sick and I started to bleed badly. I called Holles Street and they told me to come in straight away for a scan. The pain was low-grade and present in my groin and I had never felt so desolate. Albie was back in London. We had plans for me to move there. I was scared and bereft. My mother and my friend came with me. They put us in a waiting room. I waited, like the heron again, still, but not with any sureness. When I couldn't be with anyone, I went off to the toilet to stare at the wall. I had a voice tell me, 'This isn't over.'

But my humanity couldn't rise above the pain. I went into the scan and the operator had just had her lunch. There was a Hula Hoop on the floor. She ran the tracer over my belly and said, 'Is the pain here?'

I nodded, yes, and felt myself get ready for the news.

The news was: 'Large fibroid. Everything else is fine. Two heart-beats.'

I put my arms around her. I told her that I had always known I would have twins. My mother said, 'Yes. She always has.' My friend, who had made the journey twenty-one years earlier, is their godmother.

I couldn't pick girls' names. I just knew they were boys. I couldn't take it in when they told me the pregnancy was high risk. I just knew they would be born. I couldn't take it in when they told me that I would deliver well because I was so fit and so healthy. I knew it would be a nightmare. I did everything I could but they had a hellish start. I loved them all the more for it. I knew who they were before they came and I know them now. Hosios Loukas had given me a new reality. I knew I had to have the courage to follow the message then and lost friends and reputation by leaving my marriage. I took up the challenge.

There is no alternative when the message is that strong.

They came – the boys I had played with as a child. My own godmother told me, when I told her about the psychic's vision, years previously, that my grandmother and great-uncle were not the only twins in that family. Twin boys had died. They are not on the 1911 census. So they must have been stillborn or died in their early days.

There are more messages in my life, from people who have left before me. I rely on one relative, who was close to me as a child, to get through. He has never let me down in his new form. I never ignore him. These are my early days. I expect to fly. Mary T., who features in the introduction and in the chapter 'The Unnamed', gave me some beautiful words that speak to my condition at this time. In her book *Praying the Women Mystics*, she quotes a prayer poem of Mechtilde of Magdeburg:

> *You have the wings of longing.*
> *You know the pull of hope,*
> *You feel the flowing of desire:*
> *So why not soar?*

1

Angelic Histories

At the beginning of the journey the question is: why has the phenomenon of angels become so prevalent in Ireland? What need is it answering in the Irish psyche?

This is a book of spirit and a book of journey, two ingredients in which Irish storytelling takes root. The earliest voyage story is that of St Brendan. He is a father to the stories of spiritual journey and their merging with secular, although no less mystic, imagination. Stories of our nation all involve the quest for more than discovery of new places: they involve the discovery of selves. Most of these tales involve water, as a symbol not just of physical voyage but the deep unknown, the waters within us to navigate.

As I write I am looking at a print of St Brendan, peace made, setting sail for the death shore. Our first recorded spiritual voyager, our saint of navigators, returned safely only to leave life. The paradise he had found within himself could not be contained by any one shore. His story encouraged scores of monks of the sixth century to emulate him. The print of Brendan is part of my angel journey, the talisman of a trip my partner organised to give me a break from it all. He booked us into the Angel Hotel, close to the Stained Glass Museum in Ely, Cambridgeshire. Directly across the road from the hotel an artist, Maz Jackson, was exhibiting her work on the voyage of the Irish saint. It had just arrived from Norwich Cathedral, where it had hung in the biggest extension to a cathedral for six hundred years. I bought the print because it shows the saint setting out again, despite his safe return. He knew the journey to be more important and his soul yearned for the island of his great quest.

Brendan was a man of magical qualities, who discovered deity in himself and in the world. A man of angels and encounter.

This is a book of encounter, mostly of people, but firstly of some of the literature and attitudes surrounding angels in sacred text and legend.

You could argue that in Ireland we remained faithful to Catholicism in its traditional form for far longer than other countries, that in calling on angels we are seeking a replacement for that sense of belonging and adherence. But is there a deeper answer than mere obedience? We are people who prize story. The story of angels, both in our culture and in Biblical culture, is magnetic: repelling when similar ends are placed together – the Church is uneasy about angelic interests – and fusing when opposites are placed together, the angelic and the human.

It's difficult to summarise millennia in one chapter, but we can take a broad look at the history of angels, its roots and influences in pre-Biblical eras and civilisations. The Irish attitude to the literature available on the messengers of God, which was often marginalised by hierarchical dictat, was distinctly different and indicates the roots and influences of our modern interest.

Our highly-bred imaginations were drawn to the disputed texts that did not make Biblical status. These books are known as 'apocryphal', or hidden. The Bible is a collection of books known as the canon. The word canon comes from the Greek word *kanon* which means a ruler or measuring rod. Canonical works are considered authority, or the word of God; apocryphal works are disputed for their fantastical and sometimes subversive content, ideas and messages.

This was not something the early Irish monks and scribes were put off by. They knew the hearts of their own race, full of cycles of legend, full of heroes. The word *file*, poet, was also the word for seer, one who has prophetic or oracular gifts. We valued stories as much as we valued God. Monks trying to convert our wild pagan inclinations to a Christ vision needed the assistance of the apocrypha's more magical content. To wean us away from Celtic gods, towards an unseen deity, they needed the help of the visions. Then the monks themselves were woven into the fabric. The Brendan story. The Colm

Cille story. The Patrick story. So many stories of wandering men of God. So many miracles conducted by them and befalling them.

You can take the stories literally and if you expect this, you may be in the wrong book. In all the books I have read, in all the people I have met, the experiences are quiet and little publicised. People have seen things but they are not inclined to put bells and whistles on them and shout loud of their conversions. The people of this book go about their lives and look for God-touched moments. Many have had them. But the magic, as with Brendan, a man who lived and breathed and went before us, is within themselves. In telling me their messages they shared their souls with me, for which I am grateful. I always left a bit of mine with them. Each contributor gave a gift as they offered me their vision. The Brendan story is full of symbolism and the stories in the pages that follow are the same. There are moments of a supernatural nature but that is not the important thing: the important thing is the discovery in the ordinary details as well as at the extraordinary times.

The word for vision in Irish has even become a name, *aisling*. We are in love with visions. Our stories are full of them. The apocrypha feature ancient works such as the *Book of Enoch*, which was rejected by both Hebrew and Christian Bibles and is populated by angels and voyages. Superhumanity, quest, crisis and key interventions are the very basis of Irish legends.

According to Muireann Ní Bhrolcháin's book, *An Introduction to Early Irish Literature,* early Irish saints and scribes: '...were prepared to read and record the apocryphal texts that were frowned upon in Europe. As a result, more apocryphal texts survive in Ireland than in any other western European country and some of the sources go back to the Gnostic gospels and the literature of Egypt.'

Apocryphal works, those not contained in the canon of Church teaching and writing, are primarily Gnostic in nature. The Gnostics were a group of early Christians who believed that they possessed a secret knowledge. Secrets and stories, combined, are an unbeatable lore and lure for Irish people.

The revival of storytelling in Irish culture and practice has been one of the great arts to come out of the Celtic Tiger period.

The wealth departed but it left the stories behind. This is no longer confined to rural and Gaeltacht areas. In many libraries you will now find new *seanchai*, storytellers, properly trained, recounting their new tales but also the ancient ones. A friend who is pagan and soon to celebrate her handfasting with the love of her life is employed in the recounting of stories, not just for children but for adults.

We are the first generation not to rely on storytelling in some form in the home but our oldest citizens still have a physical recollection of fireside, of Fianna, of fairies and ghosts, lost times and comings and goings magical. My maternal grandmother believed in the banshee and never combed her hair after midnight in case she attracted her. She also 'put a ghost out of the house', by saying her prayers and pointing to the door at the one time. Now such beliefs are regarded as silly by some and dangerous by others, put down to a lack of education and superstition.

But Yeats, our Nobel Laureate and most famous *file*, believed in spirits and spirit world. If you were to describe him to a stranger you would not use the words 'ill-educated' or 'superstitious'. He spent the last years of his life perfecting his own *aisling*. *A Vision* was not only a poetic work but a view on the cycles of life and death and the afterlife.

The Irish acceptance of apocryphal texts is easy to understand, given our strong storytelling tradition. It is this story mindset that I think angels appeal to. Fionn Mac Cumhaill hurling boulders into the sea to create the Giant's Causeway differs little from the superhuman strength of Samson, who has a similarity to a number of pre-Christian legend strains – notably Sumerian. Rather than smother the wellsprings of folklore the early Irish Christians appropriated them. *The Book of Invasions* features a tale where the son of the King of Ireland meets Moses and Moses commands that his homeland be freed of snakes. Saint Patrick's snake-expelling reputation won the day, but like all 'truths' there are several versions.

Naturally, given the subversive nature of books like *Enoch*, there is an hierarchical distrust of angelicism and just as naturally there is a popular desire to embrace it. We love the subversive. We love the mysterious and we also want to connect with what is unseen. Angels assist. Angels appear at dramatic moments in the Bible. But only

Michael the protector, Gabriel the informer and Raphael the healer are named. It seems that angels, while evident in canonical literature, are peripheral to hierarchical requirements.

But creative expression embraces them. The same themes of Edens, of fantastic journeys and magical intercession at times of crisis, of demons in pursuit and angelic rescuing of heroic figures, are found in all of folkloric literature as well as in Biblical. The twelfth century *Vision of Tnugdal*, written in Germany by a monk called Marcus, according to Ní Bhrolcháin's book: 'sets the template for Irish and non-Irish material during the following centuries. It includes elements which must have come from singularly Irish, Christian, pre-Christian and apocryphal sources.'

Tnugdal lives in Cashel and lies dead, but for one warm side of his body, for four days. When he regains consciousness he has been to heaven and hell in the company of an angel. He gives away his possessions to the poor and paints a cross on his clothes. The story shows the confluence of Irish and Continental European sources and Eastern and Middle-Eastern text. This proves that truth is a broad term and malleable. There are so many versions of everything: even the books that comprise today's Bible vary from Protestant to Catholic to Christian Orthodox. Angels fly through all versions, however edited their final appearance. Why?

Perhaps because when things fall apart we will look for the magical to give us hope. Hope in darkness is the prevailing theme of angelic histories, whether specifically Irish or Biblical. Looking at the history of the Jews and how the manifestations of angels fitted the times they lived, the crises they went through, is a key to understanding the angel's ageless affect on human consciousness. Wherever there is magic there is dispute. And angels are much disputed. There is even one reference in *Genesis* to the men of God taking women. Such intercourse is considered blasphemous, yet there it is: 'There were giants in the earth in those days; and also after that, when the sons of God came in unto the daughters of men, and they bore children to them, the same became mighty men which were of old, men of renown.' (*Genesis* 6: 4)

A casual glance at the *Book of Enoch* will determine why the expanded version of this event didn't make the canon. It is ascribed to Enoch, the great-grandfather of Noah. It is not regarded as scripture by any group except the Ethiopian Orthodox Church, which to this day regards it as canonical.

Its older sections (mainly in the *Book of the Watchers*) date from about 300 BCE. It is in the *Book of the Watchers* that you have angels, asked to watch over mankind, failing because of the love they feel for women. They are sent to earth to beget children who become the Nephilim of *Genesis*.

How does this premise differ from Niamh Cinn Óir luring Oisín to Tír na nÓg? Genders reverse and there is a lack of progeny. Niamh is the immortal, Oisin the mortal. But the principles are the same. To a modern reading, many of the *Old Testament*'s tales are allegorical and based on oral storytelling traditions from pre-Christian cultures. Literal belief is not required. But people literally believe in angels: they arrive through the door of imagination and stay in the house of faith.

The Norman invasion brought a more standardised, stringent and guilt-ridden version of Christianity to Ireland. The divorce of the sexual from the spiritual has been one of the greatest shames in our religious development. Not for a moment am I suggesting that angels truly begat supreme beings: that kind of thought-process isn't far from following eugenics. What I discovered in reading was the magical, sexual power of some of the apocryphal texts, the very female potency. And it is a shame we cannot hold on to this as one of the centres of our human power, one of the angelic things about us.

Even in Norman times, in Ireland, the appropriation of shamanic practices had to be accepted to bring the people along to new ways. Almost all Christian wells, now dedicated to saints, had names and magical properties that were pagan in origin. The irrepressible nature and magnetism of Irish culture, of belief in magic and in stories, is capable of absorbing most religious rituals and gaining from them insight and inspiration. We appropriated Christianity to our own ends in early days; now, in later ones, we may well be doing it once more.

We are more global in our viewpoint, much as the early Irish

Brendans were when they went abroad to work as scribes and educators. Many modern-day European universities were once cells where Irish monks worked with their scribes. Is this not magically real? Our golden minds, which formed that period and assisted in the education of continental Europe, were open to mysteries more literally inclined races were already closing down on. No wonder we needed corralling by the Normans and subsequent rulers into faith practices that could be controlled, into celibacies and orders, into inquisition and hierarchy.

Now the times are opening up and the methods of spiritual expression are opening with them. It is a period of change. Of course all change brings bandwagons. Donagh, a priest and writer, warns about the desire to disappear into the need for apparitions in the place of true inner experiences:

'The loud garish ones will always have more hearers, but it doesn't mean they have more to say. They probably have less. As the world becomes more dangerous every day, many join the flight into a magic world. My fear is that they see physical sight as superior to spiritual. It's worth remembering that when people wanted to see signs, Jesus said, "No sign will be given to this generation."'

Jesus performed his fair share of miracles. Still, this is an important point from a man who has spent years not just studying but being present to spirit, whose Brendan voyage saw him living in twenty countries, under canvas in the west, in Zen monasteries as well as Dominican communities. The people of these pages, the Irish people, who have had messages, are not interested in selling their stories, only in telling them. There were lots of beautiful moments where our lives opened up to one another, where small miracles took place and life wove its magic all around us.

Bernadette, an angel-workshop facilitator whose story appears in this book and whose workshop I attended in the course of research said: 'Call them angels, if it fits, call them something else if it doesn't. It's all the one source.' This is the concept mystics refer to as one-ing, the mountain-top all faiths meet on.

The magic I describe and the magic those I encountered describe is inner magic, with powerful properties but no puffs of smoke.

Materialism was a distraction for a couple of decades but the Irish still believe more in magic than in rules. From the earliest fragment of the *Vision Tales,* a journey of Fursa which dates to 649, to modern workshops where participants are guided on meditations to meet their angels, we have been asking for help in our crises and receiving guidance. Fursa's soul leaves his body when he is ill and with the help of an angel passes through fire, returning with a physical scar to remind him of his journey.

Why ask for angelic guidance then? Why not rely on people or directly on the God you believe in?

Something is helping us. Each time I stopped on this journey, I started again, because of an angelic message that came from another human being. From a stranger I met on a mountain-top, from an artist who dedicated herself to the voyage of Brendan, from a scholar who sent me a tape of a song called 'Calling All Angels' by Jane Siberry. *Roswell* fans might remember it from the 'Christmas Carol' episode. It was the sound track to Max healing children in a ward. A moment of imagination but as real as life itself to journeyers looking for sense in a senseless world. This is what all angels do when called: they provide inspiration at moments when the spirit contained in the word is needed and is invoked through prayer.

Angels are as old as religion and older. In Islam angels are Malaekah, light-based creatures, created from light by God. Believing in angels is one of the six articles of faith. In Hebrew they are mal'akh.

Angels in Judaism, according to Rabbi Geoffrey W. Dennis: 'play a prominent role in Jewish thought throughout the centuries, though the exact meaning of the word has been subject to widely, at times wildly, different interpretations.'

Even within the same Biblical story, interpretations vary.

'The woman came and told her husband, saying, "A man of God came to me, and his appearance was like that of an angel of God, most awe inspiring. I did not ask him where he was from nor did he tell me his name."' *Judges* 13:6

'And Manoah said to his wife, "We shall surely die, for we have seen God." But his wife said to him. "If Yahweh had desired to kill us…He would not have allowed us to see all these things, nor cause us now to hear about these things.'" *Judges* 13:22

The struggle between intuitive faith and traditional religious practice can be examined in these passages. A woman, not named, who will be the mother of Samson, is advised to prepare for conception. Up to this she has been barren, a common Biblical theme. Sarah, Rachel, Rebecca and Hannah all shared the same fate and had some measure of angelic intercession to alleviate it. They are all named. Manoah's wife, Samson's mother, is not, a fate she shares with most angels. She is praying out of desperation, framed by the times and her own circumstance. A barren woman is cursed.

Whether you view this story as literal truth or symbolic parable, the difference between Manoah's reaction and that of his unnamed wife is simply this: one believes; the other has to be persuaded to see the vision for himself. Then, once his desire is granted, he fears the vision, while the unnamed wife embraces it. One does not feel the need to question; the other asks the angel his name and in a later passage is told that it is too wonderful to hear.

I've spoken to people who have had the same experience and express the same faith in it as Manoah's wife. There is a chapter called 'The Unnamed' in this book, which centres on the female experience of church. As the philosopher Blaise Pascal, who has a computer programming language named after him and had two visionary experiences in his thirty-nine year life, wrote: 'The heart has its reasons which reason itself cannot understand.' (*Le coeur a ses raisons que la raison ne connaît point.*)

No journey is spiritual without agonies and doubts. Spiritual experiences are hard to define and harder to write about. The retelling can inhibit faith rather than add to it. How can you write about an event that is beyond words? Only by having faith that the message will come through, the sense of this increasingly fragile concept we call divinity. We call out in our darkness to whatever is there and the answer comes. We tell others to increase their sense of the divine. We are being assisted and we tell others our stories to assist them when their faith wanes. So we too become angels, giving messages from our own lives to improve the lives of others. In this way angels are both divine and accessible to ordinary people, who so often feel powerless. As Bernadette says of her own angel journey, which began on a beach walk: 'After the beach enlightenment my life changed and took on a whole new prospective. I live, feel, think and act differently. I realised I have no control over future events or the events or mishaps in other people's lives.'

As if to confirm this, the early angels appear in the Bible to the disenfranchised and disregarded: Daniel in the lion pit, Abraham with a knife to his son's throat on the mountain-top, Esther on the eve of her people's annihilation in battle. The first person in the Bible to be visited is Hagar, a pregnant black slave.

Dorothee Soelle, the great German theologian and scholar who died in 2003, writes of this concubine of Abraham: 'Hagar has had to sell her body all her life, not just in servitude but also in maternal surrogacy. She flees through the arid desert. "The angel of the Lord found her." (*Genesis* 16:7) God's messenger follows and talks to her. The black slave girl is the first person in the Bible to be visited by God's messenger. His command is harsh but in keeping with her chances of survival.'

She is promised that her son will be the father of a great line. Ishmael is the father of the Arab peoples. Following his birth he and Hagar are again rescued by an angel from death in the desert. God: 'gives heed to affliction'.

Hagar and the unnamed wife. One a rented womb, the other an empty one. Both powerless in their time but made powerful in their legacies through angelic intercession. Brendan stories for womankind. Harsh journeys but great discoveries, great consequences. As with many folklore and Bible stories, there is no happy-ever-after in the lifetime of the sufferer. One will remain a slave and the other will see her son denied by his own race and sacrificing his life to bring about the fall of the Philistines.

Throughout the centuries this is the role of the angel as God's emissary: to shine a light on the greatness of humanity, not to alleviate suffering, to help the human carry the mortal burden, not remove it. To read angelic histories is to read torment, first for the Jews of the *Old Testament*, then for the Christians in the New. Inter-

estingly the *New Testament* makes no mention of angels at the birth
of Christ. But artistic depictions of the most celebrated birth the
world has ever known show angels in attendance at the magical
moment of nativity.

Angels are both mystic and tangible. They have a power over
our imaginations that has crossed all ages and professions of
faith, not just Christian or monotheistic. Monotheism means
one god. Religions worshipping multiple gods perhaps have no
need of angelic intercession. The minor gods of Hinduism and the
Bodhisattvas of Buddhism are all present to listen to the specific
request of the life pilgrim. In my home I have a statue of Guanyin/
Kuan Yin, the Bodhisattva synonymous with mercy and compassion,
usually female. The name Guanyin is shortened from a wonderful
term, Guanshiyin, which means: 'Observing the sounds or cries of
the world'. Not unlike the angel who took heed of Hagar's afflictions.
The Islamic mystical poet Mansur Al Hallaj wrote in the ninth
century:

> *You were my true friend in the day*
> *And in darkness my companion.*

This is the role of angels. We are, as the modern mystic poet
Ivan M. Granger puts it: 'the individual separate from the eternal'.
The angel is the bridge across that chasm. The darker the time, the
more we need messages from spirit. Angels are present at key Biblical
moments. Yet they are treated with some suspicion, even fear, by the
religious and scholarly hierarchies.

Still we expect them to fly and we, the ordinary people and our
imaginative brethren, the singers, poets and painters, the novelists
and dramatists, worship them for it. From folklore tales to sacred
texts, from canonical works to apocryphal, these divine beings are
present to us and with us. Their role of messenger remains but their
guise changes in the course of the Bible and other religious visions.

The Jewish *Talmud* marks the change in appearance and need,
from sky-filling to quiet words, from flaming to whispering:

'Up to this point [400 BCE] the prophets prophesied through the

Holy Spirit; from this time onward incline thine ear and listen to the sayings of the wise.'

Angels in the gospels could be easily be interpreted as humans. They have no need of power but are announcers of events.

From the shadowy beings of the early books, to the supernatural descriptions of Gabriel in the *Book of Daniel*, to the more human man in white advising of the Resurrection outside the tomb of Jesus, angels are journeying with the progress of the people they guard and govern. After the birth of Jesus angels disappear for a time from the *New Testament*. There was no need for emissary; God became man. The divine took on human form: Jesus, worker of miracles, comforter to the oppressed. Only upon his death do angels reappear: 'Do not be afraid I know you are looking for Jesus.' (*Matthew* 28:6)

In the early books the shape and appearance of angels are not described. But from the sixth century BCE the literature around them becomes more epic in nature. Angels acquire names and faces. At this time the Jewish people are slaves in the Babylonian empire. Never have they felt less chosen and more forgotten. So a hero emerges, a Daniel:

'Then I lifted up mine eyes, and looked, and behold a certain man clothed in linen, whose loins were girded with fine gold of Uphaz:

'His body also was like the beryl, and his face as the appearance of lightning, and his eyes as lamps of fire, and his arms and his feet like in colour to polished brass, and the voice of his words like the voice of a multitude.

'And I Daniel alone saw the vision.' (*Daniel* 5:7)

This is the time, of profound spiritual crisis, when angels are first given wings, a spark of inspiration that can likely be attributed to the winged gods of Babylon. For the Jewish people to be freed from slavery, their intercessors must have the same power as their captors' gods. Angels never sleep: they watch over the chosen continuously and, as well as giving messages, they protect. In this way they awaken the broken spirits of the lost people.

By 538 BCE the crisis is over, the Jews return to the Holy Land and the rabbis, afraid the worship of angels might threaten the undiluted word of God, are refusing to include the journey of Enoch and other apocryphal works in the final version of the Hebrew Bible.

Later Daniel's angel with the face of lightening and feet of flames will transmute into the softly spoken man in white, at the tomb of Jesus, using the *Talmud*'s wise approach to angelic message. The people are still subjugated but no longer enslaved.

By the time *Revelations* is written, persecution is the order of the day for the early Christians. Archangel Michael is wielding his sword and the four apocalyptic horseman mount their steeds. Christians are in the lion's den. A full circle of fate back to Daniel, favourite of Babylon but slave of Babylon, awaiting deliverance, needing angelic intervention. Just as the Jews looked to the angels in times of trials, so do the early Christians and they too require more than celestial telegrams. The *Book of Revelation* sees angels carrying out retribution against unbelievers. Michael is fighting against forces of Satan in *Revelation* 12:9. A third of the human race will be wiped out (*Revelation* 9:15)

The book of God's word closes. The role of angels continues. In the early centuries of Christianity, first the apostles, then the early monks and saints meet angels on their spiritual road, which often concludes in martyrdom. Paul meets God on the road to Damascus. Peter is led out of his cell by two angels who put the guards to sleep. St Vincent, patron saint of Lisbon, is roasted on a gridiron in the fourth century. He is visited by two angels who fill his cell with flowers. Martyrdom is made easier to bear. The prospect of celestial assistance, should there be occasion for you to sacrifice your blood and bones, helps you feel less forsaken.

Decisions about angels become important work. They continue their metamorphosis, based on the influences of the time. Perhaps because so many possible works featuring angels were rejected, thought turns to developing what can be allowed, what is angelic hierarchy, making reference to Biblical verses. In the fifth century, *The Celestial Hierarchy* is attributed to Dionysius the Areopagite, although he may well not have written it. It gives the classifications that have become part of tradition: Angels, Archangels, Principalities, Powers, Virtues, Dominions, Thrones, Cherubim, and Seraphim. Cherubim and Seraphim are typically closest to God, while the Angels and Archangels are the closest to human affairs.

The lack of an authoritative doctrine of angels does not hinder belief; it offers a window of opportunity for people themselves to decide how they wish to see them. Popular imagination demands them and artists supply celestial images, music and stories. No church is without them, no society. They permeate every strand of culture, from popular to highbrow, from Sistine Chapel to saccharine love song, from poet to pop lyricist. We respond to angels, rather than reason as to whether they exist. They are the best part of ourselves, the journeyman in Brendan and in all of us, who wants to pursue ideals rather than mere realities.

As a result they appear everywhere and nowhere. Great minds of medieval times meet to discuss how many angels can fit on the head of a pin. The argument centres on whether angels have bodies, or, as we see in art from the fourth century on, whether they are winged. The Middle Ages bring new interpretations and conceptions. Thinkers put angels under intense scrutiny.

In the thirteenth century, St Thomas Aquinas, regarded as the greatest and last of these medieval philosophers, called Scholastics, explores the notion of the role of the guardian angel. And a new component of faith, already a folklore, becomes a doctrine. He decides you can have guardian angels, of individuals, of family and nations, of situations and events. A hundred years earlier the female mystic Hildegard of Bingen is giving her vision of angels to an artist to draw a mandala form. It's a non-hierarchical view: the angels form cosmic circles around a white centre, an emptiness into which all your thoughts and meditations pour; the white centre is the mystery of God and the mystery of you.

Companion or champion, teacher or servant of your needs – the view of angel depends how you wish to perceive it. This is the one thing that never changes in all the centuries of changes.

Today there are thousands of angelic names and functions. The recently published *Watkins Dictionary of Angels* has more than 2000 entries and its compiler, Julia Cresswell, acknowledges: 'There is a general agreement that the number is vast, if not infinite.'

She tracks their emergence in apocryphal works, their limited appearance in the Hebrew and Christian Bible and the *Koran*. Another important source of angelic material is the group of books known as the *Pseudepigrapha*, a collection of books attributed to people who feature in the *Old Testament* but not written by them. Many of these sixty-five books contain visionary tales: the *Markabehah* and *Hekalot* follow the same storylines laid down by the visionary tales of Ireland which we began with. *The Book of Enoch* is also part of this grouping. The *Kabbalah* of the Middle Ages developed out of *Pseudepigraphia* mysticism. Books of magic and conjuration are also source material for angels.

The medieval angel is not quite the visual we have today – it is covered in feathers for one, as many surviving images depict. The wings on human form arrive with the Renaissance painters and sculptors. This is the angel of our modern imagination: an angel formed on the brush tips of Botticelli, Raphael – named for an angel – and Da Vinci.

And what of the angel of our modern day experience? What does our belief in angels reveal in ourselves? People are feeling vulnerable and uncertain. There is a need for protection and a link with the old times, before the fall of magic. A fascination with angels is a belief in the spirit of ancient times. The revival of interest meets scholarly scepticism and is considered anti-rational. Some quarters consider it dangerous. But the angel shops spring up and the workshops fill.

Whatever our reason, clinging to the old beliefs or making way for newer, more expressive and individual forms of spirituality, angels bring messages for those who believe they do.

The chapters that follow discuss this. Some encounters involve seeing, others hear, others meet their higher selves in forests, others get advices in the chance comment of a stranger. However the message arrives, it has helped the people in these pages into their changes.

My journey began with the written histories of angels, but in the words of St Vincent Ferrer in his *Treatise on a Spiritual Life*: 'Consult more than your books.' The journey that began with me consulting my own past and the messages that informed it broadened to encounters with others and their messages.

3

FORGIVEN

This is a story of forgiveness. Bernadette knows more about it than I will ever know.

On the way to the chip shop to get our Friday-night dinner, in the absence of anything edible in our fridge because I am talking to anyone and everyone about angels. My son says. 'Our dog is called Angel and she does nice things and that makes her an angel.'

The *Talmud*'s advice comes back: 'Incline thine ear and listen to the sayings of the wise.'

I've tried workshops and angel evenings. They're enjoyable and have some moments of what might be enlightenment. But they're cabaret spirituality. Performance art dressed in niceness. There's a lovely smell of incense at them and a sense that the real is not really present. I just don't believe what I am hearing at them either. Give me a sign, Lord!

On the chipper notice board is an advertisement for an Introductory Day with the Angels, with Bernadette. I call her and tell her about this journey.

She says, 'You're welcome to come along. I have nothing to hide or prove.'

She is in her middle forties and has worked hard since she could walk. She found her way to truth and a life as a practitioner after the kind of darkness we never want to experience. But I don't know this yet. I just hear the honesty carved out of experience down the phone. And I breathe a sigh of relief. Whatever this woman offers, it will be authentic.

Bernadette says on the phone: 'The energy I work with is angelic, but it's all from the one source. The angel name serves the purpose of giving people something they understand. But the healing goes beyond understanding. I have felt the power of God and of forgiveness. I'm not a massgoer. But I walk the beach in front of my home and I pray every day. I get my answers.'

I remember thinking: beach walk. A great way to pray. I also recalled a monk telling me, years ago, when I was trying to be holy and go to mass but not getting anything from it: 'Your God is in nature and silence. Go out and meet him.' So we have something in common.

Bernadette works with an angelic energy called 'Integrated Energy Therapy'. Within a few minutes of meeting her, I think she doesn't need a system. She is a woman of great personal power, an angel in the way she encounters and welcomes people, in her most beautiful home by the water. She has created so many dreams from nothing, it's no wonder she helps people to realise their own as part of her life's work. She has no trouble encountering the rebel in me and we like each other. I admire her forthright nature. Within a few minutes I am jotting down, in a workbook she supplies me with, what the monk said, and also a phrase I heard from an artist who came into my company for a short while. Her name was Claire and she loved to wander. Her heart ended up in Africa. She looked at a picture I'd drawn and said, 'You're a no-house person.' `

It was an unusual comment for someone to make to their landlady. She was moving into the house I was renting out. And accurate in a way she couldn't have realised. I lived in Australia in the back of a car and the desert of the Northern Territory was my happiest home.

I forgot Claire's message. I write the words in capital letters, under Angel Raphael, the healer, who clears illusions of separation. *No-House Person.* And I tell the group something about myself I had lost in recent times. I tell them about the free-spirit artist who left a pearl in my head, along with her rental deposit. But I don't say her name. No wings, no chorus, just a sense that I have reached a powerful truth. I also write: *This is good for your children. Houses aren't everything.*

In Bernadette's beautiful palace of dreams I find that I have no need of one for myself. My home is in my children's eyes. When they're grown I'll never live under one roof again.

As the day draws to a close Bernadette talks about a painting behind my head. She says the artist moved to Africa. It's Claire. I have seen some of her murals on the walls of the house I rent out. But her charcoal drawings have an altogether different quality, an abstraction that makes the figures, one adult and one child holding hands, symbolically real, rather than recognisable. The figures are heading for new territories. And the drawing is as much about loss as about the discoveries. Moving towards any truth is liberating but you are also liberated from comforts, from nests.

I leave the day with a definite feeling that something profound is being pointed out to me. My dream for myself is a little restored. Destiny is just the next day in any life. I have begun, for the first time in a long while, to look forward to my months and years ahead, with story in them. We can be angels to one another.

I come back to Bernadette's home some months later. When she begins to talk I have no idea I will learn so much about forgiveness. She is going to tell me some of the messages she received and the U-turn in her life seven years ago:

'I'm no archangel's right-hand man or woman. Not interested in that kind of ego. I came to my spiritual practice out of my own pain and awakening, not because I was special but because I was human.'

'I was a busy mother and businesswoman, busy daughter, busy to everybody. I've always had angels in my life, don't know whether I called them angels. But I've always had a knowing, from the time I was a small child. I was always the one in the family looked upon as "weird", the knowing one. The aunts used to say they were "worried about me". Though I didn't realise what they were worried about. But now I know I had ability to prophesise, which used to terrify them. I could say something off the cuff in the middle of a conversation, wouldn't even know where it came from. Then I couldn't understand what I know now.'

What kind of things did she foresee?

'I knew when people were going to die, I saw in dreams where they would be buried. Then I'd know things that were going on in people's lives. It wouldn't have been possible for me to know it and I'd say something that related directly to their private issues. Once I told my parents, when I was a young girl, that they didn't need to worry about the money coming for something, it would be there. They had kept it from us children but at the time they were very worried about money.

'I was very close to my grandfather and I saw where he would be buried. I saw it was going to be with a baby that he and my grandmother had buried. I saw the baby. I thought that baby was in an old graveyard and that there was no room for my grandfather to be buried in it too. But when I walked in, my uncle and my grandmother were discussing the funeral arrangements and that was where he was placed.

'Then I had to let go of it when I became a mother because life intervened. I was afraid of it all and didn't want to know this was part of my life. I was so busy rearing my children, struggling to make ends meet in the Ireland of the 1980s. It was a wonderful time because everyone had nothing. Then my husband came up with the business idea in the 1990s. Michael has never been out of a job since the day I met him. He is very clever. We had the opportunity to work together and we got a lucky break.'

I'm not sure about her use of the word 'luck'. When I see Bernadette I see a woman who has gone every inch of the way herself, determined to make it and making it determinedly. But she was not in her right life, even at the top of the tree.

'I wore the business suit grudgingly. I hate technology and the business environment. But I was good at it.'

Together Bernadette and Michael rode the crest of the boom wave. They worked all around the clock and it was then she realised success is as much pressure as struggle:

'The hardest part is that while you are trying, you have an aim. Then the dream becomes a reality and it's hard to stay there. You build up a reputation and it has to be maintained. When you get to the top of anything you're teetering. You have the responsibility of people in your employ.

'When, in the 1980s, we owned a car you could see the road

underneath in, we thought about when we would make it. It was the dream that kept us happy and warm. Then we got it and we had to realise all our years and effort had been put into making it, without a thought of what would happen when we got there.

'I was six months in this house when I came down the stairs one morning, I'll never forget it, for the longest day I live, I came down and realised: "I'm not cleaning this beautiful house for somebody else. This is mine. Wow." Bernadette sat down with this knowledge, and thought about what getting the dream had meant: 'I had to go back and think about what life really means. I had to think about how much we had sacrificed.'

Firstly, in the years of managing her workload and family responsibilities, she had developed an aggressive form of arthritis:

'This arthritis is very debilitating. At one stage I wasn't even able to dress myself. You can be crippled with it. I had to put up with so much illness and pain. Within months I went from being a totally fit young woman to being on my knees. I lost my confidence in myself and my body. With this arthritis you can wake up fine one morning and in so much pain the next you won't be able to stir out of the bed. I used to cry with the agony.'

She prayed that something would come along, that the family wouldn't suffer or the business be put in jeopardy. Then a miracle happened. She won what we describe as the arthritis Lotto:

'I was under a wonderful professor and told him my life philosophy: "I want quality, not quantity. That goes for whatever drugs you can give me too." He remembered that comment, bless his heart and soul, and when a new treatment was introduced in 2005, he contacted me. I am one of the lucky few who was on it and it changed my life. My pains had gone completely. I was able to believe in my body again.

'When I got my health back I realised that the business was never my dream. That was my husband's dream. I supported it. I took my first sun holiday and realised that I would never ever go back to the everyday grind. I hadn't had enough time or enough clarity to develop my spiritual gifts.'

There is a point, when people are telling you their story, that you think you've heard it, that it's time to ask the wrap-up questions and thank them for their gift of time. But then a silence happens around Bernadette. I know it's not over. It's not that kind of silence.

'We had everything you could dream of, but tragedy had struck in another way…'

As she begins to tell me, I have to ask her to wait a moment. My brain races to catch up with the events she is describing. If it had happened to me, I don't know how I could resurrect my faith in anyone or thing, let alone in the universal energies she is convinced support us:

'We learned that my son had been abused by my paedophile brother. I trusted him not all of my life, but *with* all of my life. How my son became so abused was out of my brother being seen as a good son and provider for his widowed mother. And my son was a favourite grandson.

'A grandmother fell totally in love with her grandson and loved to have him to stay with her. John was the apple of her eye. She would pick him up from the house and bring him to the family farm. It's the most normal thing for you to go to your grandparents over the holidays and at weekends. I did it with my own grandparents.

'My brother, while I didn't particularly like him as a person, I never had an issue with him. He was abusing my son for years under my nose and my mother's nose. John never said a word about the abuse until he was twenty-one. I knew there was something wrong when he was growing up. From sixteen years of age on he got into drugs and drinking, didn't finish school and couldn't hold a job down. All the classic signs of abuse were there. His behaviour had my husband Michael and me blaming each other. He thought I was being too soft on John and I blamed him for being too hard. But we had pinned it on the wrong people. When you don't know anything about abuse it's very hard to see it.

'I see it now but I wouldn't have seen it then. It's a blame game. Paedophiles rely on the parents blaming themselves when their child starts to act out. They start the abuse when the child is young enough to feel it's their fault and they continually tell the children it's their fault it's happening. My son was subject to sexual abuse and rape in every way imaginable. It's certain he would not be alive today, he'd have killed himself with drugs and drink, if my brother had not had his own son. When that boy was three-and-a-half John couldn't live with the idea that it might happen to him also, at the hands of his own father. He decided to be honest about what had happened to him

'From the minute he told it, he was heard. I went straight down to the house to confront. But my mother refused to believe us and supported her own son. I supported mine. I didn't doubt for a second. I knew it had happened. One thing about my son: he was in trouble but he never told lies. He doesn't mince his words now and he didn't then.

'I knew my son needed me now, to help him on his healing journey, I always knew if he healed, we would heal with him. It was his choice and his right to prosecute and I supported him the whole way. It was the only reason he came forward. He didn't care himself whether he lived or died. He just wanted to protect the next wave of children in our family. I am so proud of him.'

The details are horrendous. There were almost sixty counts on the abuser's indictment for his trial but after consultations between the prosecution's legal team and defence counsel his guilty plea to eighteen was accepted. The judge imposed nine concurrent terms of ten years, eight concurrent terms of four-and-a-half years and one of two years. He will be in a prison for a long time. Bernadette was there for the entire proceedings:

'You sit in a room and watch the jury of men and women crying as the counts are read out. Then you look at the face of the accused, who is your own brother, who had done this to this human being, to this child of your own, with no remorse, you begin to wonder if it's possible to believe in anything any more.'

This is the feeling I am grappling with as Bernadette continues:

'We had to lose the beautiful moments, his father and I. All the memories we had built up over the years of rearing our family were destroyed. I had to revisit them again, knowing this was happening to our boy at the time.'

During the trial she glimpsed her mother:

'He was meant to be sentenced that day. There was a room in the Four Courts. We were brought to wait there with the detectives, the barrister, solicitor and so on. My back was to the entrance and John saw her pass by. He said, "Mam. It's her." I turned around to see her going in to speak up for her son.'

The sentencing wasn't carried out that day but Bernadette was now under one of her own:

'Something broke in me that day. Something finished in me. I broke down. I could see why she was doing it. She was defending her boy like I was defending mine. But almost everyone else by this point had seen it. If she had only seen it too she wouldn't have died so alone. It's very sad that my mother's sons could not do any wrong from the day they were born. I was the eldest girl and I saw that clearly. Even though they did wrong, she couldn't see it.'

She carried herself on a journey towards acceptance. She left that courtroom and came to a place where she could forgive. It took all her strength:

'It's so important. Your precious life that you have created, protected and nurtured, is being violated by your own blood. I was the mother who would see trouble before it ever happened. But in actual fact I didn't see what was really important.'

This is where I contradict her. She was a victim also, of deceit and betrayal. She spreads her hands and says:

'I was manipulated into the situation. I see that now. But at the time it was hard to get my head around. The depression. I can't tell you. I knew counselling wasn't going to help. I needed the help of God, not an employed professional who moves on to someone else after the hour is up.

'With the help of people I have met, people I know were given to me by spirit to get me through, I got through. I was so ill six months after the trial.'

Suddenly her beach walk becomes more than a great thing to do. It was the only thing to do that kept her sane. Each day she walked answers into herself:

'I walked that beach, you have no idea how much I walked. I asked God to help me. I turned back to God. I wasn't a massgoer and I'm not going to be either. I had to turn to the higher power that is. No psychologist was going to help me through this, give me the answers that I needed. I felt so worthless as a mother because I felt that I had allowed it to happen.'

Her walking shifted her body, which had begun to stiffen and ache in all the trauma, and her deep intuitive nature came to the fore. She brought it out of childhood. She became a child.

'On the beach, I had a feeling my mother was there with me, in spirit. I was going along that beach, suffering with depression. I was struggling so hard. I remember thinking: 'If I don't forgive these people I am never going to be able to move on myself'.

'I realised there and then that this was too big for me. I had to forgive my brother and my mother. But this was too big for me. My mother was still alive at this point. Then there was a moment, where a voice came to me and said, 'You don't have to forgive them. This is not your job. Leave it to a higher power.' I felt this wave of peace and relief travel through my body. This feeling that I was being minded was all about me. It was over in a few minutes but it changed the way I do things, entirely.

'I never looked back from that day to this. That was beginning of my release.'

But, as she explains, forgiveness is a process. It took time and more work. Her dreams became very vivid and held images and scenes of herself and her mother:

'She had to engage with me and I had to engage with her. There was a peace about us before she died. It happened through the dreams. I physically remember every single dream. The ones where I ran from her. The ones where I fought with her. Then one night it changed. We were in a room, the two of us, sitting on a couch, at opposite ends. We were talking to one another, turned towards each other like this.' She crooks her arms and her hands hold the position of the hands around the heart of a Claddagh ring. 'When I woke up that morning. I knew something significant was going to happen. Next thing my husband takes my phone from me, as it's ringing. He would never normally do this, he'd hand it over to me.

'"Michael, has Mammy died?"' I asked him.

'I got my breath back. Then I said, "Bring me to my home place. I want to see her and be with her."'

'I never thought I would be able to do that, and I never would have if it hadn't been for what I felt on the beach that day.'

I realise that what Bernadette describes is the same as what everyone I met on this journey does. They describe peace, love, relief and a sense of being cared for. A sense of being a comforted child. No matter how these moments arrive, they share the same characteristic. They are god-touched.

'I was the one who buried my mother. I dressed her for burial. I cleaned her house and sorted out her last few things. I wanted to bury her with dignity. My brother was not allowed out for the funeral: he was on remand. She had died within two months. He broke her heart. She was broken.

'I cried. I said to her, "I'm sorry about the way things had to be." My mother is still in my dreams. She is with me more now than she ever was while living.'

Bernadette continued to walk the beach, faced with the truth that her mother had died still denying her son's trauma, died still defending her own son. Her brother was in prison, her mother in a grave. There was physical evidence of her mother's intentions to betray her grandson and Bernadette herself:

'When I was sorting through her possessions after her death I came across a copybook with what she was going to say to the judge that day. She was going to ask the judge to have mercy on her son because he was the only child she had left to look after her.'

She has, with the help of her source, found a way to continue the process of forgiving her mother and even her brother. Not his acts, but his soul:

'My mother died tragically. There was a freedom for me attached to that death which may sound cold and callous to have experienced. Grief-stricken and all as I was, I knew that I was free.'

Six months later she had her first session of IET, angelic healing.

'I knew before the end of the first session I was there to let my brother go. So I booked to come to see this woman again. We had lived with what he had done constantly for two years. He was behind bars. What came to me the second time was that there was nothing he could do to my son or my family now.

'But I still felt stuck. I continued to go back and gradually the weight lifted off my shoulders. The weeks after each healing took away that weight. I began to walk straighter and think more clearly. I had to realise how much guilt I was carrying – for my son and what he went through, for my mother's pain in her family falling apart, even – and this is the crazy thing – my brother ending up in prison. I would have left no stone unturned to see justice done. But I grew up with this brother of mine.'

She had an innate sense of loyalty and she was the only person who was not benefitting from this. It was time to care for herself, as she had never cared for herself before. On the advice of the woman who was giving her healing, she signed up for a course:

'I often thought about my own abilities in this period, my psychic abilities. Like the dreams with my mother. I had no doubt we were doing in spirit what she wasn't capable of doing in person. Our souls, our other selves, did sit together and put to rights what had gone wrong. I never saw myself working as a healer. I knew I could explain a lot to my family about what we had gone through.

'I was only learning for my own use. I wanted to get closer to the angels, my source. I was not doing this to become a practitioner. I am a hermit by nature. But I wanted to know. I worked with friends and family, people I knew wouldn't laugh at me. They took to it. They began to feel the benefit in their lives. They told other friends and family.

'I began to realise the vulnerability of people. They handed over their money in blind faith. I began to realise all the charlatans out there. I started teaching because people kept calling on the phone and I knew how vulnerable they were, because I had been myself.

'No matter how sceptical people are when they come through the door, it helps people to see the roads they're meant to be on. My purpose in life is to help other human beings see the power within themselves. They can reach it for themselves.'

Bernadette realises the human mind cannot conceptualise wholeness. We might need angels initially as a means to grasping the divinity. But we are all part of the same oneness, wholeness and source.

'I bring people together for a day. I give them an opportunity to meditate, experience energy. If they let their minds go, they will experience that energy, find it for themselves. They don't have to look for the outside world, it's all within.

'The only sure thing is that we are alive today. The rest is blind faith. People are drawn to the word "angels". They're at sea, they have no control. It's all for a reason, their suffering. Call them angels, but that is a man-made word. I know there is a god and god is within. We use angelicism as a concept to help people get closer to them. We are all equal. We are all healers. Before I work with a group I always remember the higher power is not the teacher or facilitator, it's the hidden. People need to take back their own power. The only way we are going to do that is to look inwards, to listen to ourselves.'

I left Bernadette, full of the silence that falls when you are taking in realisation, full of her journey. This is a story of forgiveness. Bernadette knows more about it than I will ever know. Or ever hope to.

4

The Unnamed

The best student goes directly to the ultimate,
The others are very learned but their faith is uncertain.

Yongjia Xuanjue (665-713)

'Good women have no history. How women prayed, how women thought, nobody remembers. Almost any woman we know of is an aristocrat. We have so much work to do to find who we are and where we have come from.'

Mary T. is referring to women's lack of power within the organised church, which is reflected in the lack of historical and theological documents by women. There is a lot written about women but usually in response to something they are doing, or are considered capable of doing, that the organised church is not sure about. It is not something she lets hold her back. Her studies and writings in the area of women and Christianity, her particular love of the women mystics, have given this woman Christian a lifelong passion to bring whatever history, whatever stories are available about women of faith, to light.

I've come to see her because I have a sense that the rise in interest in angels is primarily amongst women. The one thing I did get from the angel cabaret shows I attended, without success or benefit, was that a handful of men and hundreds of women attended. The representations of angels for sale in angel shops are 90 per cent female. The historical and Biblical indications of angelic androgyny – or maleness if any sex is to be put on them – is ignored. The angels in my house are all female figures. I wonder if this is related to the fates of women, such as the unnamed mother of Samson, to the good women who have no history, to the powerful female need to be heard and seen in spiritual gatherings and practices:

'Nobody gives away their rights. They have to be taken,' Mary T. states in a very peaceful manner. There is no stridency in her tone or practice.

When I mention this, she says, 'Pacificism is inevitable if you're a feminist.'

Perhaps the quiet growth in interest in angels is a peaceful revolution. The women of faith are looking for a way to be what they are naturally. To be themselves. Throughout history, if they had the courage to do this, they risked death or persecution.

I've also been bending the ear of this blazing, brilliant woman on my lack of qualification in the area I am writing in. I have no religious or theological qualification. I have no experience.

'Human divinity is part of a woman's life. You know everything you need to know, from yourself you know,' she is quick to point out. 'One of the things I like about the women mystics is that they say it's for everybody. The men mystics, at least in the Middle Ages, make knowledge and intelligence the most important things. "We're most like God in our intelligence." The women mystics say: "We're most like God when we love."'

The women mystics were a group of fabulous, forthright, motivated and fiercely loving women who lived in Europe in the Middle Ages. Their contribution to time was both rich and rare in our spiritual history. The medieval period is associated with darkness, torture and repression. But out of darkness came the pearl sound of women who didn't want hierarchy but wished to be involved with the people, to speak and write in their vernacular languages, of their visions, their prophecies and their ecstatic experiences of God.

Mary T. determines four periods in the Christian history where women flourished and the medieval period, when the women mystics wrote, composed, drew, spoke, healed and lived, is the great time. Their writings were often suppressed and they with them. But eight hundred years later their accounts of God, their visions and contributions, have huge relevance.

Julian of Norwich, Hildegard of Bingen, Margery Kempe, Teresa of Avila, Marguerite Porete – we know some of these names. The version of God these women sought was non-punishing, loving and close to the people. Some of them survived persecution for such ordinary ideals. Others, like Porete, were burned. They all incurred inquisition. But they continually spoke the truth. Their visions, particularly those of Hildegard and Julian, are still written of and spoken of today.

Mary T. is a scholar, born to be a thinker and to evaluate, yet she never asks once to read what I have written. My version of her is not her. But this is what I think of her. Listening to her I found a church I never knew I had. I listened to her stories of women, such as the Beguine, who organised themselves into self-sufficient communities and did not take vows, which would have given them male hierarchy to adhere to, but who counselled themselves and lived a spiritual life in the company of other women.

It comes to me: they are women without orders. Even the word 'order', which we use for the various groupings of nuns and priests, says so much about control.

Mary T. doesn't see why an ordinary unordered woman cannot go on an angel journey. This is not the privilege of academics and trained religious:

'My growl is that they confuse information with wisdom. They know everything about everything. It takes years to know who you are and what is going on and what truth is. And in some ways the less information you have, the better, because it's just a distraction. Define expert. I have a thing about experts. In Canada, where I spent most of my religious and academic life, an expert was somebody who came from Toronto with a briefcase. That was an expert. And I always came to class with my stuff in a plastic bag, just to say, for me, education is reciprocal. I used to say this to the students and it scared the daylights out of them, "I have to learn as much from you as you learn from me. This is the transaction here." I know more about the Middle Ages than most people I know but that's irrelevant unless it somehow resonates with something in you. You know, there's no point in talking about it.'

I am trying out my idea on her that messages from humans are as powerful, as generated, as wild fantastic visions. That every journey is an angelic journey, because every journey involves new messages which will and can change your life course.

'Exactly.' She's handing out homemade cookies. 'It's an invitation to a new journey or to continuing on the one you were on.'

I tell her about some of the big messages that have changed the course of my life.

'And that's really important,' she responds, 'because there's very little literature like that. Angels should not be about money-making. I've been told I'm being superior about them. There's absolutely nothing I need to know about people with wings. My mother, anything she knew about prayer, it came from here,' she points to within. 'I think prayer is a human need. I don't mean saying rote prayers. Just basic attention to reality. Just being attentive.'

I'm excited now, chiming in with her: 'Then the voice that comes to you out of that reality, gives you another step.'

She nods:

'It can happen in dreams and it can happen anywhere. Or it can happen in a conversation.'

'Or you pass someone on the street, and you hear a snatch,' I'm adding on, just as she asked all her students to. 'Or somebody addresses you in such a way that you know that you're hearing more than what they say.'

'That's right. Or for me in reading. I read a lot. On dark days I have to have lights and I have a magnifying glass and all sorts. But on days like today I can read easily and that's why I love these days.'

I hope this doesn't upset her but I have to say to her I really wonder that the three or four people that I've met that have had a real effect on me spiritually are all going blind.

'Maybe because we're all older,' Mary T. laughs. 'I'm in a sort of stasis at the moment. I have to be really careful at night. I don't want to fall and I don't want to die from falling. And please, as a favour to me, as a favour to yourself, stop feeling you're not an expert. You're an expert in you.'

'I agree I'm an expert at following my instincts. And eating biscuits.' Now I feel we're like Pooh and Piglet. That most reassuring of relationships. Worried Piglet, kind Pooh. Except Mary T. has a big brain.

Talking to her is great fun, even when it's about awful things, like being left stranded in a different country by the religious order she was a member of, because she would not agree to sign a document that unanimously voted to reject short-sleeved blouses. Like just after this, when her mother opened the door of her Irish home to her daughter for the first time in seventeen years and said, 'My God, what have they done to you?'

They didn't do it forever. She went back to Canada to face them, went on to become an eminent theologian and scholar who has written a three-volume history of Women and Christianity, who is a world-renowned expert in the women mystics and has compiled a volume of prayer-poetry, *Praying with the Women Mystics*. She's Professor Mary T. if she cares to be. And she makes fantastic cookies.

I want to know what her take on angels is, before I get to the story of her incredible life, loaded with messages. I tell her about a key event in my life. How I got a hunch if I made a phone call on behalf of one of my family to the person who had rejected them for a job that was vital to them, it might reverse the decision. Previous to this hunch, I had heard a little voice inside myself saying, 'You're a child of God.'

'That's not my kind of language now, Mary. It's just not. My first answer to that voice was, "Eff off!" I am at pains to tell her. 'But then he got the news, which I knew was devastating for him. So I looked up the interviewer's phone number and said, "I'm not speaking to you as anything other than one child of God to another." She gave him the job he's still in. To me this is an angelic message. How do you say that without sounding certifiable?'

She's looking at me. I'm being encouraged to answer my own question. So I say:

'I have to say it. It's the truth. The only thing that matters on a journey like this.'

'Exactly. My friend Shirley was into dreams a lot. She made me learn watercolours, basket-weaving, all this sort of stuff to try and use the other side of my brain. But it takes me a long time. She used to say, "Pay attention to your dreams and listen to whether you're awake or asleep in your life." It's like learning a different language.'

'It's the language of instinct. And the instinct is more than animal.' I follow her thought to my own place. I think of Bernadette and how much Shirley and she would have to say to each other.

'Absolutely. And, it's what keeps us alive. Our instincts are what keep us alive.'

'Where would you go to read about angels, if you were me?'

'I wouldn't read about angels. It's a symbolic word for messages. That's what it is. I would never pick up a book. I'd pick up a book about dreams maybe, or being attentive, being integrated, sufficiently integrated. I'd pick up a book about mysticism. My definition of mysticism is praying with integrity. Praying with integrity is being true to myself and not trying to use somebody else's language or put on somebody else's spiritual cloak or something. It's trying to be faithful to myself.'

This feels good, this feels close to me and any of those whom I've talked to so far, that I related to. I do think you can get huge messages in your dreams. They tell the truth you don't want to acknowledge. I tell her I've been having a recurring dream, of being pregnant and never giving birth to the baby.

Mary T. shoves the cookies nearer my reach:

'Wow. That's this book, probably. Don't be high-falutin', she advises. 'I have so little patience for that. Actually, there are two people writing my biography at the moment, in Canada. I'm waiting to find out who I am. I keep giving myself liberties now that I'm in my seventies. I gave a talk from the heart, about what I found out in my life. I've found out that there's a woman tradition in Christianity which is totally different from everything else. My own life parallels the story of feminism in Christianity. I got bored saying it, so I wrote about it. I'm still getting emails saying, "Do you have any more copies?" It just goes out and in a way, I don't mind, because I think knowledge is free. Should be free, I don't think you should have to pay for it.'

When Mary T. left the convent she wasn't going to get married, so they gave her 5000 Canadian dollars:

'We used to say, "Chastity is worth five thousand dollars."'

It doesn't seem a lot for seventeen years' service, devoted service. It's just that she wasn't devoted to what they thought she should be devoted to. They wanted obedience:

'I never got the knack of obeying people.'

Her future husband called her the most immoral woman he'd ever met. But then, when he first met her, at a prayer group meeting she was visiting, he thought she was a plant from the bishop. He told her, 'Sit there, say nothing, just sit there.' Then she spoke. He liked what he heard and asked her out for dinner. She flicked through her diary and said, 'April?' Six months ahead. He thought it was a brush-off until he got a phone call from her asking if their dinner was still on? In April. They got married quickly and had seven happy years before he died of diabetes-related illnesses. Her mother died in the same week. She herself got cancer that year: '1987 was my year.' It occurs to me: had she stayed in cloister, had she not been mistreated by the order she gave her life to, she would never have known the experience of pain, of risk, of vilification and of being outcast that characterised the lives of the women she has studied. Experience over knowledge, her life has been an echo of theirs, but they don't burn people in the town square any more:

'It's such a contradiction in terms to be a woman Christian. Women haven't been allowed to say what it means to them. In fact, they have been absolutely forbidden to say. There were four outbursts of women in history. Women in the year 55 were told they shouldn't speak, they shouldn't teach, they shouldn't think. That was it. So they were excluded and it was possible to write the history of Christianity without ever mentioning women and still is. And it was possible to do theology as if only men could think. And it still is. All theology is male theology.

'I started researching and I found, in the fourth century, a whole explosion of women who just couldn't take it any longer and became virgins to escape marriage. That meant leaving marriage and living henceforth as a virgin. We have some writing from them. And then they were wiped out. Then the Middle Ages came and it was the most misogynistic time and this is when the women mystics exploded.'

It's always a reaction to repression?

'It is. And the more it gets centralised, and the more it gets organised, the more it gets to be about power, up come these women. Women are at their best when society hasn't settled down. During wars, for instance. They left Christ's tomb and they were the ones to say, "It doesn't end here. It has to continue."

'We have three hundred years (1150-1450) and that's where we have the most writing from and it's incredible. We have about three thousand pages of text. It's poetry and it's prose and it's absolutely brilliant, and they learned to be human from looking at the human. They didn't care about the divinity of Christ, they cared about the humanity. Why were they looking at that? Because they needed to know what it was to be human, because everyone told them they weren't human, they were subhuman. Okay, so they had to be a bit pious to keep from being burnt at the stake. It didn't save many of them. But that's the kind of phrase they use. It has to continue.'

It has to be by the people, for the people. The burnings weren't just burning bodies, they were burning their ideas. Mary's books might well have been burned for their beauty and their truth. They are about women claiming their own history and their own tradition, trying to make a consecutive narrative out of all that experience that was never recorded.

The groups of women I have been visiting and joining in with may be about the very same thing. They are gathering in rooms, under the auspices of angels, but actually to relate to each other as spiritual beings. The visions, the things they see, are just the same as the great visions of Hildegard of Bingen. They put their story minds, their female minds, to spirit and they see things beyond themselves. Just as Catherine does in the chapter called 'Coming Alive'. She had a real experience, of letting her daughter go. A vision to last a lifetime. An *aisling*. It is inspired by her power as a woman and her privilege as a spiritual being. If you put the visions into the heart of your life, your life regenerates.

Mary T., being an academic, is more literal in her interpretations. She is definite that the women mystics were having symbolic thoughts rather than visions. I am a story woman. I have no problem with the visionary aspect. She sees it like this:

'I'm not in a trance, and I'm not out of myself. It's just I'm giving my brain room.'

In 'New Rooms', female brains are being given a chance, an opportunity, to come alive. But I feel there is more to Bernadette's experience, in 'Forgiven', more to Martha's in 'All My Relations', more to the two Catherines in 'Talking to the Dead' and 'Coming Alive', and more to many of the experiences you will read in this book, than brain room.

I believe mortals can have moments that are immortal. Having seen so many changed faces, shared so many long talks, I know spiritual experience is beyond brain room. But it does not have to be otherworldly. You can have a magical moment without the use of magic. I don't think the moments of this book are magic-induced, I believe they are soul-induced. They are the stories of grounded people. The fantastical versions – and I heard many of those – just did not belong on these pages. They were part of the angel journey only to enable me to discount those who crave magic over spirit. Spirit belongs at a kitchen table as much as at an altar. More so, in my view. That is why the groups are forming around them and people are gathering to speak to one another's condition.

I am so excited. To know Mary T., to be one of those witnessing the rebirth of belief into something so human and approachable, so kind and so welcoming, so wise and so equal. These are the characteristics of the angel journey and Mary T. is one of its mentors. But, of course, you have to know pain and suffering to be able to communicate with everyone as an equal. Part of Mary's suffering story, part of her prayer, was her decision to leave religious life. She had been sent to Canada when she took vows and hadn't seen her family for years. They had sent her to represent Canada at a worldwide meeting of her order, known as a chapter, in London. That was where she refused to sign the blouse document, which needed to be an unanimous agreement.

Her mother's response to her physical state was echoed by her response to her mental state when she grasped it. The years and the reaction to her within her own community had taken their toll on

Mary T. She decided, after resting in Ireland, to return to Canada and to make ready to leave the order:

'I went back to Canada. There was a big meeting of all the people for us to report what had happened at the chapter. And a message came that I wasn't allowed to address it. It was a big meeting hall beside a church, so I went over and sat in the church. I was crying again. And I knew then I had to leave. I said to the superior of my house, "I'm going to leave but I don't want to leave broken. I want to stay around. I won't interfere." I knew if I left at that stage I might have a breakdown. I was teaching at the University of Toronto so I would have had my job to do. She said to me, "Try and fit in as much as possible with the house rules. And please don't use petty cash to buy a car." Because the way the vow of poverty was then, there was a little box. If you needed toothpaste you went and got your money. And apparently some of those who were planning to leave were saving up money that way. It would never have occurred to me. I wouldn't have been that organised.'

She was organised enough to produce a magazine for her order, which had great ideas but it was decided the magazine was too radical:

'I was upsetting the simple faithful. Which meant I was making them harder to rule. There were twelve who helped me produce it, twelve.'

I think immediately of the twelve apostles.

'They each got a letter saying, more or less, it's either Mary T. or the community. And they said, obviously, we're going to go with the community. Some of them came and told me but the others I didn't know about.'

One friend stood by Mary T. She is her friend to this day. Bríd, another Wexford woman, now eighty-seven, walked away from religious life after thirty-three years. You will meet her in another chapter. For now, Mary T. has this tribute:

'Life was made very difficult for her. Bríd was the reverend mother of a boarding school which was about two hundred miles out in the wilderness in a glorious place. She was a very creative teacher. She used to get the native Canadians in to teach the kids earth lore.

What they did to her, when she refused to sign the letter, was that they stopped the money in the bank. The bank manager said, "There is no money." And she said, "But I've a hundred and twenty boarders to feed." She went back and phoned some of the farmers and they all brought in food.'

There's no mercy in that kind of decision: that the order was prepared to let children go hungry to make their point about obedience.

'Absolutely none,' Mary T. agrees. 'It's power. And it's not being willing to let your power go. After my year mucking around in the convent I said, "I'm leaving now." My superior said to me, "But you've been so good the past year, we thought you'd settled down." They totally misunderstood the point I was making.

'By that stage, four of us realised that we were making the same journey together so the four of us met and we moved into a house together. The four evangelists. We became a halfway house for troublesome nuns!' She laughs.

Ironically, after she left, Mary T. was much in demand as a scholar with theology departments. They didn't want her. But they wanted the learning:

'I fitted their need and I was being called a distinguished teacher. I was writing and one of the essays I wrote was named the best essay that year in Canada so they were getting a lot of kudos from me. It worked very well.'

She became a noted historian of church history, she married, but Mike, her husband, became seriously ill:

'He had renal failure and he stopped dialysis. He also had triple amputations and the whole diabetic thing. He wanted to die where I was going to live so it suited us to move to Waterloo, which is about an hour outside Toronto. And then he died in November.

But this is not her last resting place. She found her people on her journey and now lives in Wexford among them:

'My people are my family. I've come to know my family. And my people are the women mystics. Actually I'm closer to the women mystics in some ways than I am to others. Bríd is one of my people. Shirley was my people. There are a few other friends in Canada.

Former students too. So every now and then a former student will come to my place.'

Where is that place?

'The place where women pray. I need to know how women see God. And I need to know how women experience God. That's where I want to be at the moment. And that's where I am and I'm having a ball.'

Mary T. is part of the air I want to breathe. I go home with extra biscuits and a charged heart, a book of *The Illuminations of Hildegard of Bingen* and reason to carry on. I see, as with all the people I encounter, a different way to her, but she has brought flashes of brilliance, colour and context to my mandala.

I am thinking, as I drive home, with a seventy-five-year-old teddy called Yeah strapped into my front passenger seat, that I am like a child again. The teddy makes the journey to and from school with the children. I make the journey to and from Mary's house and come home with a two-thousand-year female spiritual heritage and her definition of God ringing in my ear:

'It's the other side of awe. That's God. It's the mystery of love that holds the universe together.'

I've also left with the message that my feeling of being ill-qualified is the exact reason I should be the one on this journey. There is no knowledge standing in the way of experience. Maybe this is an opportunity to be kind to myself and have a kinder sense of spirit. I wonder if this is the god the women in the angel rooms, the women of the new rooms, are seeking.

5

NEW ROOMS

Mary T. is chiming still:

'We have so much work to do to find who we are and where we have come from…prayer is breathing with the planet…women are at their best when society hasn't settled down…'

I find a lot of groups. A lot of women are meeting in the new era of faith in one another's living rooms, at another's kitchen tables, to organise, not a new religion but a new affinity. They accompany one another on issues of faith and spiritual practice. In sitting rooms, the extraordinary is being discussed.

I am sitting in Marianne's room, in front of her visionary board. We are taking up all her sofa and we are laughing but there are so many tears. She is a nurse working in a frontline unit that deals with overdoses and other hard cases. Street people and lost people all benefit from her work:

'I try to do more than nurse. But lately it's been so hard. I never get sick but I am ill now.'

I think it's less an illness than an overburdening. Marianne is a giver. She and her husband support their extended families, back in South Africa. He lost his position as a deep-sea diver, after a terrible accident. They lost their home and had to rebuild their dreams. Day by day they did this, in faith that better days lay ahead.

They came to Ireland to make dreams. The way life fell they had to send their only son back to South Africa, which has left his mother grieving. She misses home. She misses her son.

She gave no thought to herself or her needs. Then life caught up with her and demanded that she rest. She had no choice. She and her friend meet in each other's houses and have begun to work with angels. Asking for help to get things I take too much for granted. A roof over her head. A chance to live as one family again. On the visionary board is the oath she swore when she became a nurse and she has kept it to the letter. Her board is full of pictures of close family whose future she protects. They have sent cards thanking her for being an angel. As her mother writes: *You are so much more than a daughter*. Every cent counts. There is nothing left over. Marianne gave so much for decades. Now, she realises, it has to be her turn.

One of her signs was a flower, which grows in her homeland, of which she pinned a picture to the board. A friend, knowing she was sick with the need for her family, to see her son, for the tastes, sounds and sights of her country, called around with a plant for her. When it grew it was the same flower. Common in South Africa and rare in west Dublin.

If ever a woman was a flower, Marianne is one. Strong, fragile, scented with kindness, blooming after retreat, blossoming out of dark.

The new rooms, with the new way of seeing spirit, keep women afloat, giving them kindness and comfort and messages that they are not alone.

During the journey I was invited to several gatherings and got to most. I came away from each one well nourished in all manner of different ways. This is Spirit in the City, a gathering where women share their most intimate concerns and experiences. Importantly, the people who come are affirmed, not alienated, by feeling that they are less than they should be. The spirit at these meetings is always one of welcome.

In every gathering, everyone has a story relating to their spirit. I keep thinking of how many more unshared stories are out there. At the gatherings there are no priests. No leaders. Pot luck dishes and hospitalities. Laughter. Sharing of gifts. Support for trouble. Praise of breakthrough. These are the characteristics. One gathering I think I won't make is in south Wexford where my close friend meets others to speak of the truth they find in one another's company. I have three separate arrangements for the Saturday it is scheduled for. So she tells me about what she calls the happening:

'We needed a new kind of Sunday. So we have these weekend meetings, once a month, to give each other Reiki and talk about what matters.'

All three of my arrangements fall through. By chance or design I end up in the village my friend lives in at the time of her gathering.

Today there is a male friend with them. A Reiki master. He gives me a Reiki session and I realise, half-way through it, that my ragged breath smoothes. Mary T. says prayer is breathing with the planet. My prayer grows calm. By the time I've spent an hour on the plinth I am free of the tearing sound and I can hear my children playing outside. I remember Iris, a woman who appears in 'Coming Alive', telling me to listen out for the sounds of my children's laughter.

In the kitchen the women are drinking tea and speaking of the times they live in and the changes in their existence, marked by their desire to remain in spiritual spaces but in ways that fit rather than detract from their personal power. They talk about things they could not speak of in a church context but with other women have no issue passing on. This is intimate faith, free from rules and rites.

Siabhra talks about how conception came hard for her, with echoes of the times of Sarah, of Hagar, and the unnamed mother of Samson:

'After three years of actively trying for a baby, having numerous invasive tests and a laparoscopy, just around the time I turned forty I was about ready to give up. I had a pain in my chest constantly which was, I now realise, a hard knot of grief and sadness over having missed the boat where children were concerned.

'I had begun to accept that this was the way things would turn out, when I visited a very gifted medium for a reading. She immediately described my father and told me he was with me and zeroed in on the conception question straight away.

'She fired off a series of instructions prefaced with: "Your daddy says…" They were quite specific. I was to lose a bit of weight and get very healthy. I was to go to an IVF clinic in Galway where there was a particularly good doctor and I was to get moving straight away.

'I live in Wexford and had exploratory surgery in a hospital in Dublin so the idea of going to Galway made little or no sense. I was also in dread of the expense and the sheer ordeal of going down the IVF route but I simply followed instructions and made up my mind to act on the advice. My long-suffering partner who has two grown-up children and who had been patiently enduring as many tests and examinations as I had, agreed immediately to go along with my seemingly mad decision.

'I rang the clinic tentatively to book an appointment. I told them I had heard good things about them (I didn't name my sources), and that I wanted to make an appointment. A very kind woman explained that they were very busy and that it could take up to six months to fit me in for an appointment. I digested this and was still debating whether I had lost my sanity when she phoned me back ten minutes later to say that they had had a cancellation and seeing that I was so nice about them she could fit me in for a preliminary consultation in ten days' time.

'I felt elated and terrified and a bit bewildered but oddly filled with a sense of the rightness of this, of the way being cleared.

'In the meantime, on the advice of a very spiritually attuned colleague in work, I had been given the name of an energy healer after an uncharacteristically stress-filled outburst that overtook me at a meeting. I was in such a state that I treated this as a priority and managed to get an appointment so I went to see this woman and explained my situation. She immediately honed in on my ovaries and told me that one was blocked completely and the other was very lazy. She worked on my feet and with my energy field and explained that I now had some chance of conceiving.

'A few days later, one Thursday evening in February, I took the train to Galway with my partner. We had an appointment with the clinic the following morning. I was uneasy because my period was due and I was expecting it to arrive any minute and was worried that it could interfere with the tests and procedures that lay ahead. However, all went well: we attended our preliminary appointment, had a very pleasant overnight in Galway and came home.

'The following Monday my period had still not arrived and, on the urging of my partner, very reluctantly, almost as an afterthought, I rummaged around and found my last remaining pregnancy test with the old sinking feeling of: "Here goes, nothing again."

'It was positive. I remember sitting in the kitchen holding the test kit and feeling such a sense of gratitude and grace. The way I looked at it, what I needed to do was to trust and relax, which was what I managed to do when I turned over my efforts to a power greater than myself. I felt led by the hand, almost at times, banged over the head because I can be a bit slow on the uptake!

'In November of that year we had a beautiful, healthy baby girl who has lit up our lives every since and I am sure my dad is pleased I followed instructions – for once.'

Mary T. speaks of this, how this birth experience, this mystery, has never been used as a source of theology. She maintains that human divinity is part of a woman's life and Siabhra's story, given to other spiritual women, in new rooms, talking of spirit in new ways, is part of this continuum.

Donagh, a Dominican priest and philosopher, whose thoughts and guidance feature in the chapter 'Angel of Friendliness', touches on this:

'The real tragedy of Christians in the last few centuries is that we turned the Christian faith into endless explanations. Anyone coming from another world would think the basic affirmation was "The flesh was made word", and not the other way around. There is a fleshly core to the Christian faith and it is missed when we try to be spiritual in a way that ignores or denies the body. Then, as for some modern visionaries, it's not enough to return to that ordinary physical base; we have to look for extraordinary physical experiences.'

Siabhra doesn't regard her physical experience as extraordinary. Her impression is that women's wisdom and the energy practices combined to give her the gift she was seeking, to be a mother: 'We're almost afraid to talk of this. We shouldn't be.'

Wherever I go to join the gatherings, there is something good to eat and something good to hear. I think of the early weeks, when I joined with an angelic sergeant-major who demanded to know the angelic nature of all the feathers we encountered. But in the less structured environment of like-minded friends, almost always women, the talk is freer and reception of it less tense.

Betty hands me a cup of green tea and one of the brownies. They taste better than transubstantiated communion. She adds her story to the line of thought that is spiralling out of all these meetings:

'There are times when you need the help and no matter how practical you are as a person, you have to reach out for what's not in front of you.

'In November 2004 I was in hospital for three days in Naas to have my gallbladder removed. It was a Tuesday. I was to have an operation the next day. There were other things going on in my life at the time and I was anxious enough. I was sitting on the bed, facing the door. All of a sudden, I'll never forget it, the four corners of the room were filled with beautiful balls of light. The first one came in over the door,.

'I was fascinated and I thought, "Can everyone see them?" I used to be a nurse so I had the sense to think of whether I had had medication. No pre-meds or anything like that. They converged over my head and spun round me. They danced in front of me and were gone. I knew I was going to be all right. They were there to tell me it was going to be okay and I wasn't alone in this.

'I watched them coming from the corners, watched the dance and then they were gone. It must have been over in seconds but it felt like hours. After I got out of hospital I knew I was going to be okay with all the other things going on. I knew I was being looked after. Up to that point I had experienced a lot of loss. My realisation was that if things were meant to happen, they would happen. I learned to say before I went into something, "Is this going to be okay for me?" I would get an answer back whether to proceed or not. When I saw the house I'm living in now, the minute I saw it, on the internet, I got a feeling and the minute I set foot in it I knew it was for me.

'I am aware of stuff going on; a lot of it goes over my head in busyness. Sometimes things happen that you just have to laugh at and you have to say, "Thanks for that."

I always say: 'Give us a dig out.'

'I have never found anything scary in it. For me it's been warm and loving and comforting.'

Sarah is part of a group of women in their thirties and forties who meet once a month to share the condition of their lives. For her the group provides spiritual uplift, as well as recognition of the everyday issues. The women she sits among are strong in their determination to live well and truthfully. They are led by a woman in her sixties who believes in following spiritual principles. Spiritual sense does not always make commonsense. Sarah and her fellow group members see their gatherings as a means of meeting the divine in themselves and in each other. There is a resistance to church practice and theological knowledge and an experience of the divine. She shares this with the listening women, of whom I am one:

'Knowledge of God could take me only so far. I realised that somewhere in the act of encountering life and growing up. Somewhere between expectations and anger, joy and sorrow, laughter and tears, loss and grief, I seemed to lose that certainty of my God. It was during this recent time, when I could not know that God was real, when I doubted what I thought I knew for certain, when I did not pray because I could not pray and when I was most afraid, it was then that I encountered the experience of God. The experience of the spirit moving in my life. I did nothing special that I recall, apart from being still. In that being still I experienced God in a daily way. Everything became sacred. I truly experienced "a peace which passes all understanding". And that peace, rather than my understanding, is what grows now.

'But I do not experience this peace consistently. Uncertainty is my constant companion. Still, I wait in expectation, for glimpses.

'Living with the spirit for me means living in uncertainty, especially when I am called or moved to do or act in a way that I know will be considered odd or strange. Sometimes I hear God speaking and try to ignore it. But it just doesn't work. I find that more and more I just answer the call and amazing things have come out of listening to this call. Amazing moments and encounters that I cannot understand but I can experience them.

'Living with the spirit also means that I can see the intention behind somebody's action. It means being able to "read" people because I am seeing them from a God perspective. I said once that seeing people from this perspective and being able to intuitively feel the vibrations of another's emotions should make life easier but I find it makes it harder at times. Because I cannot turn away from another's pain or hurt.'

In Kilkenny I sit over a Friday-night supper with a group of friends who meet regularly in one another's houses. Molly, Rose, Sinéad and Norah describe their journeys and in with the laughter is a serious message. All of them are looking for a way to be free to express their entirety; all are moved to find answers to the questions of their lives.

Molly's struggle to find her way through family crisis had left her depleted and searching for answers:

'It would always be in times of crisis I'd say a prayer. But things had got so bad and my head was so messed up I didn't even have the energy to pray. I was just like, "Somebody do something, because this just can't keep going the way it is."

'My dad had had an operation for cancer and he had complications afterwards. He didn't know where he was really. And we were concerned about how his mind was going to be afterwards. A week later it was still the same; there wasn't any change.

'He was babbling away but not making any sense and we were trying to get him to come around to talking about normal things. And this man just walked into the ward, at least sixty, grey hair, really well dressed in a suit. There were four people in the ward. He walked straight up, looked in at my dad and said: 'Ah, there you are.' And he had a big smile for my dad. Dad said, 'How are you?'

'We presumed Dad knew him from work, because he said, 'There's a man who's on his holidays.' He had little cards with Archangel Michael's picture on the front and a prayer on the back and he gave one to each of us in the circle. He caught Daddy's hand and he said a prayer silently – he didn't say it out loud – while he was holding Daddy's hand. Mam figured out that he was doing some kind of a blessing and she took his other hand.

'Then he said, "We'll see you now, there won't be a bother on you." Daddy was the only one he actually stayed with. Mam was a little bit shaken by it. Afterwards we looked at Daddy and asked: "Who was that man?' He said, "I don't know."

'From that point on Dad really improved. His memory came back and he was back home with us within a week. It was huge. That evening I was up to Rose, who's here tonight, and we did a guided meditation. Different angels were working with different parts of the body. Archangel Michael came up. I just opened up into floods of tears. I knew there was a link between the man, the prayer card with Archangel Michael on it and Dad's recovery. A reassurance. A comfort.'

I ask Molly how it has been for her since, how the experience has impacted on her:

'I think that you can experience beings. They are doing things in existence, for the will of God. Somebody to give you a dig out and help you. It's strengthened my faith in a different direction I suppose.'

Rose starts to talk about the statues of St Joseph selling out around the city. People are turning them upside down and putting them into their gardens to try to sell their houses. I have read of a Celtic tradition of turning objects upside down to let the luck run back into a hard-pressed life that seemed to have run out of it. I know this is how horseshoes came to be turned up, rather than down. Blacksmiths in the Celtic world were seen as more than tradesmen. Their work was elemental, sacred. I wonder if the Celtic folklore consciousness turned St Joseph upside down. In the wider world of Catholic folk-magic, originating in the Middle Ages, he is the patron of real estate matters and home sales.

I remember the estate agent who came to my house when I was trying to sell it and advised me to place a miraculous medal in every room. A sharp-suited woman, advising of talismans. People will say so many things in private.

These Kilkenny women are kind to share their stories. They are talking about moments precious to them that could be so taken out of context on a printed page. Once more I find myself evaluating. No matter what the truth, whether the man who came to Molly's father was real or angelic, the help came with him.

Sinéad helps herself to a salad and speaks in a quiet way about the grandmother she was close to and lost:

'The memory would be the night my granny died. I was nineteen.

She had always been in my life. I was premature, I wasn't supposed to live. I was three months early, the smallest premature baby to survive at that time. No matter where we were or where we went Nanny was always there. As I've moved on in life any time something happens I always go to her grave. And I only live two miles from where she's buried.

'I remember the night she died I was asleep and I woke up and she was sitting beside me. She told me that she was okay. Things would be tough but we would all be okay. And things have been very tough. We chatted for a few minutes, then I fell back asleep. I woke up, thought of the conversation and thought, "That can't be right." I knew Nanny was in hospital. I went into Mammy and I woke her and I said, "Nanny is dead." She said, "She can't be. She was fine. We only rang the hospital last night. She's grand."

'The phone rang as we were talking, to say she had just died. No matter where I go, I always feel her. Always. I just feel so secure and loved. The energy, it gives me direction. I'd ask a question and trust the answer. I don't know where the intuition comes from but I have more confidence. I trust instinct. Okay, right, that's where I have to go. I just feel comfort. I've changed my life recently. I know she's there, helping me do it.'

Again and again, the conversations turn to comfort. And a pattern to this is that the person speaking will qualify it by saying they are not fools. Why should they consider themselves to be? Does it matter where messages come from, once they assist us in our humanity? Sinéad expresses the contradiction well:

'I would be wary. I would be very wary. I would be open but I wouldn't be, I would be very closed. I suppose that's a good way of putting it.'

Norah, who has hosted the evening, speaks softly about using Reiki for family and friends and how it has helped her to cope with her grown-up son moving about the planet. She is a free woman and wants him to be free but the question of safety is never far from her mind. A concern she keeps to herself, as do all those who are letting go of children. She has been given a deeper set of friendships and awareness from the pursuit of spirit. Rose has encouraged her to practise Reiki more. She has had some angel-touched moments, the value of these women as friends being one of them.

Rose has found the energies so valuable to her that she is moving away from a successful career towards working full-time in the area of energies. In terms of mortgage repayments, she helped a couple recently to clear their new business premises of an energy the owner was convinced was wrong.

'They've been able to meet their repayments and support their family in the past three months. I feel good about that.

'I wasn't born into it. I'm not from that type of family at all. I think the perception of this kind of thing was complete fear. But I was drawn to it. When I started to express it, it was like, "Rose's away with the fairies."'

Why is that the common belief?

'I think it's human conditioning. I think it's family conditioning. My children will be completely different now but that's only because of me. They can only go with what they know.'

Molly chips in, 'I work in a school and I do meditation with the children. They love it. You know the way you have to persuade adults and convince them? With kids it's just normal. They're so, "Yeah, cool," and they don't bat an eyelid at it.'

Rose has trained in angelic energies as one of her principal practices:

'A lot of the time when you meet adults they've tried everything else and they've nothing to lose. I work an awful lot with Raphael and Michael, because he'd probably kick me around the room tonight if I didn't give him a mention. But I always think of them as jokers. I feel they all have personalities. They're like people. It isn't all the rays of angelic energy coming down from above or anything. They're like the fairies. They like to play and they like to hide things and they like to mess.

'And they definitely like you to ask. They tend not to play ball unless you ask nicely and say, "Thank you very much." You have to be very appreciative, as you would for anyone that you show respect to. But I find Raphael's energy phenomenal.

'And I'm also finding that people who have family in spirit, their energy would come into the room. That's really special for the person who's there. Spiritually I do think you go through upheaval to get to a place of understanding.'

How has this manifested in Rose's life?

'I came to it because of my son. Our first child died, very close to birth, which was very traumatic for both myself and my husband. I would see him from time to time. And that was my first experience. My son's room, especially, the lights would flicker. He would often say to me, "Did you see Joe?" I'd say, "Yes," but I might not have seen him. It's just to allow Evan to be able to express himself.

Evan then went through a traumatic illness just after the birth of his baby sister. Rose did all she could to assist him and when the medical route produced no answers she tried holistic therapies. She went from being what she describes as 'aggressive', to being open to what happens in new rooms, in ways of being. It has made her, in her own words, 'Gentler, more accepting of others. And I think everybody now accepts me exactly as I am. I think I probably have a better relationship with most of my family. I think the more you believe, the more the spirit allows you to see and feel.'

Who was Rose before?

'She lived a very strict life. She worried about everything. Nobody would see that. Fierce, she was fierce. And don't look sideways because you wouldn't want to touch her.'

So if she was to meet herself fourteen years ago, what would she be saying to the person she was?

Rose's face lights up:

'I'd probably be saying it's better than you can ever imagine. You'll definitely have good times and bad times. And whatever you decide to do just do it with a whole heart and decide to pay it forward. For me, it's all about bringing it to more people. A gift isn't a gift unless you share it. I don't think you have to be Joan of Arc. But I think you should be able to make a conscious decision that whenever you meet someone, you'll do something in some shape or form to make their lives better. Sometimes it's just a smile. I think we all have a light and it's our job. I think we were put here for a reason and it's our job to make it shine.'

The ordinariness of a meeting of women in houses. The extra-ordinariness of their experiences. These kinds of stories must happen a thousand times over in the lives of people and go un-noticed, or are kept private for fear of reaction. I don't have the same faith in the literal angel characters the women speak of but I have full faith in their experiences and the meaning in them. Does it matter what name you put to the messenger, once you react to the message and use it in your life? I want to carry on. I want to find people who have hope where there was none. Who have found redemption. As I think it, it's on its way to me. I never expect to hear what I hear. Or to see what I see.

6

Fallen Angel

Many of the figures we now number as saints began their journeys towards God as humans engaged in reprehensible acts.

St Francis, St Augustine and St John of the Cross, patron saint of poets, all began their lives as well-off philanderers. Some were worse than shallow. St Paul extracted money from the oppressed to give to the conquerors, taking a sizeable cut for himself, before Damascus. Pre-enlightenment, you would have found these men arrogant, un-caring, cruel in their behaviour. They left children, betrayed women and took from those who could ill-afford it.

On a packed ferry last summer I met a man. He sat next to me and asked me what I was reading. John of the Cross: *The Dark Night of the Soul*. I knew he had seen the title and been drawn. There was something compelling about him, a clarity and disturbance combined. I thought it might have been the book shadowing my impression.

'I never look back, or forward, I live in the day,' he said, looking at me with what I can only describe as eyes full of honour and horror. He was hesitant: he had desire to speak and not to speak.

The past fringed and followed him but he had become something more than it. He had a presence some see as aura but that I see as charisma. He had a depth of tone and a truth to his voice. This man never tells lies, was my thought. Very clearly, he had come from being one thing to being another and his journey spoke in his physicality in a way his mouth didn't.

'You really learn only from bad things. A violent nature is either in you or it's not. I've seen violence and I've been violent. When I came home to my country I had to find a way of dealing with the things I'd seen and done.' He had been a mercenary soldier and witnessed casual executions and executed, though never casually, professionally.

'You could have someone killed for a fiver.'

I believed him. People were sitting all around us. We were not free to speak. I told him about the book I was working on. We went to a quieter place on the ship and spoke for a while.

'I would love to tell you more about what I did and where I did it but I always tell the truth. It wasn't just abroad that I knew violent people. Where I live I have been involved with violence. I was involved.'

There are people who claim their gangster connections and people who have been connected. I had no doubt of his belonging to the latter category. He became involved in another way of living and is now devoted to energy healing; he has experience of angelic energies:

'But to me it's all the one force. Reiki, Angel, call it what you like, it's tapping into the same current. I started working with this energy as a form of self-counselling. My first master told me he wasn't going to work with me any more. Then a second teacher had the same experience. It was fear on their part. Something happened. They were scared off.

'I would have had nasty experiences, living in a violent environment when I was abroad. I realised when I got home that I needed to do something to keep my mind right. I've never experienced guilt or fits of conscience. I don't experience those emotions. But the work I did before desensitised me and I found it hard to live in normality. I attracted people to me who were similar.'

He has developed as disciplined an approach to helping people as he once did to hurting them. He follows a strict code of diet, exercise and good work for the suffering.

'When people find out about the healing, they ask me.'

He does not charge. This is a man who doesn't believe in penance but in repayment. He doesn't believe in karma but he has no doubt that without turning to light he would be consumed by the darkness of his previous acts and environment. Up to the point where he returned from soldiering to his native UK, his psychic gifts manifested only when he was angry.

'I knew things from a young age, under twelve. I predicted a guy's death and within two weeks he had drowned. I blamed myself for it at the time and long after this. I would only see things when I was angry with the person. It happened again five years later: in a row I saw someone's life end and it did. He just disappeared. When I was abroad this guy, within a week of my feeling he would die, was burned alive in a car crash.'

Then, as his instinct for the good work grew, it wasn't always people whom he had clashes with whose death he felt:

'At one point I refused to get into a car with a friend because I knew he was going to crash. Then I told my wife something terrible was going to happen. Shortly afterwards he had an acquired brain injury. His mind is perfect but the body is immobile. Something similar happened to another friend. I called and said she needed to mind herself and change her car. She wrote her car off.'

I asked him how he read people and he said from holding their hand. He took my hand and told me three things. They weren't what I wanted to hear. One of them was:

'You don't know where you're going with this story yet. You're lost with it. It's not going to be easy for you to tell it.'

His manner told me he wanted to get away from me, as I did from him, but we were able to match each other in truth and response. At one point, I was terrified. Then something funny happened beside us and he laughed like a baby. All his heart came into his laugh and the gaps in his story, the curt way he headed off some of my questions, I realised they were for my benefit, to keep me real rather than nice:

'Everyone wants to dress spirituality up nicely. It doesn't like fancy clothes. It likes the truth. Keep telling the truth.' Initially he had said not to say he was a soldier, but then he said: 'You can use what I told you. But I'm not prepared to say any more.'

This summer, a year after I met the first fallen angel, I find my way to James's house easily. He lives beside my close friend and I have always been struck by his life force. When she suggested that I speak to James in a deeper way, I never expected to hear what I heard. Or to see what I saw. There is a whiteboard in his kitchen with a list of to dos. The first name on it is an addict he is helping in his recovery. The same surname and first name of someone very close to me who died tragically in recent years. I often feel his presence. This name is not a common one in Ireland.

'How many people have you met with this name in your life?' I ask James.

'One. Him. Come out the back.'

He is in his Dublin garden, which he has turned into an Eden. Soaking up the sun and life. There is a right-angled scar, running along the line of his midriff, then turning a rapid right. His new liver lies under it, pulsing, absorbing chemicals and flushing out toxins.

There are stories that a transplanted organ gives you some of the cellular memory of the person it once belonged to. James laughs and says if he were in a room with his donor, a woman he calls the Angel, she'd realise she is being brought to places she never knew existed.

'I was born in 1952, the youngest of eleven children. My mother was forty-five and my dad was fifty-seven when I was born, so it was like growing up with grandparents. But I was well nurtured and well cared for. We had a factory house in our town: two bedrooms, no bathroom, a tin bath on the wall. My mother was a really good woman.

'I was a happy child. Then I was abused sexually, around about the age of ten, a friend of my brother's. He was about sixteen or seventeen at the time. After that a series of older men abused me, on my street, and introduced me to sex at a different level, which made me feel really dirty. I took the tin bath off the wall to scrub myself.

'I remember going to confession and hedging round what was happening to me and going to communion to feel clean again. At this time I started to act out and began thieving, my mother's purse, down the shops, I was a little magpie. Anything that was glistening I took.

'I told a Christian Brother at school because I wanted this to change. I knew it wasn't happening to everybody. I had excluded myself from loads of stuff. Sport, which I would have loved, I avoided because I thought people could see through me and I felt dirty. I'd also started to act aggressively and become a nuisance and all the rest of it.

'One of the first things he did was to offer to examine me. I said no. Then he arranged a private confession for me. It felt then it was only compounding that I was wrong. Why would I confess anything? My connection with the church started to dismantle. By the time I was sixteen I got thrown out of school for being disruptive. I was clever but couldn't concentrate on anything. At sixteen my father died and I got on a boat and went to England.

'I went to London and straight away became a very mad, very sad junkie. I didn't drift into drugs. I took to them with great gusto, straight from amphetamines to heroin – and alcohol, which I had been on since fourteen. It was all because I couldn't handle these feelings, couldn't come to terms with who I was or what had happened to me. I couldn't work it out, what was going on with me or who I was.

'The voodoo of the church, that I was a bad person, had me. You're fucked. The fact that I enjoyed sex compounded the fact that I was bad. I had nobody to talk to about any of this. I spent eleven years, up until I was twenty-seven, taking drugs. In those years I was very destructive. I lived with girls who were on the game all the time. I was on the game myself. I robbed. Anything to get money. It was all about getting stoned. I always had girlfriends, didn't have boyfriends. I had sex with men for money. That excuse set me free. I didn't have to think about any alternative, like that I was queer.' His tone is wry.

'I was in a relationship with Julie, who subsequently became my wife – and still is. She wouldn't put up with any of my nonsense but she fell in love with me, why I don't know, and kind of stuck with me.

'I lost half my stomach from burst ulcers on the street over there. I was living on the street on and off. Julie got me to hospital when it started. I was worrying over a court case, because I was always in trouble. I had a two-year suspended sentence and got caught within the two years on another charge. So I was due up in court. I had this very famous solicitor, whom I had done favours for. He got me off on emotional grounds but I had to be deported into my mother's care and go for treatment. Those were the conditions. My mother had never even been into a Garda station, let alone a London courtroom. The day she came to court there was an ex-customer of mine, who was a drug dealer, present. He was a serious nutter and started screaming from the back of the courtroom, 'Send him down.' I had stolen two grand from him and a load of his drugs. He had to be restrained. They took him to holding cells and while he was in them I got my mother and legged it. It was crazy; he would have killed me.

'It seemed that I was predestined to live in madness all the time. Somewhere in there.' He points to a well-developed chest area that is scar-free. He is so vital. 'I knew it was not the life I wanted or was made for. I used to look at the life ordinary people had and long for it.

'At the end of my using I had three kids. I got married to Julie and had them. There was no thought put into that by me. It was just about using all the time and all about her trying keep it together, to hold on to me and fix me. My first daughter was born in a squat in Ireland. Then we got a council house. Then we got evicted because anything I could earn was going on drugs. I think when my third child was born, I remember sitting there one day and thinking, "This is really wrong. I would be better off not being alive. They'd be better off without me." I had done detox, been to rehab so many times but it hadn't worked. I borrowed money from somebody and fucked off back to London.

'A year later I was living with a girl called Louise. She was on the game. I was on my knees literally again. I was thinking: "I'm going to die. This is fine. She can make more money than me. For whatever reason she wants to stay with me."'

'For whatever reason' is a phrase James uses a lot. He can't imagine or define what people saw in him then. Having known him, not on this level, for several years, I can vouch for this magnetism, this pull of life, from him to others. It's impossible not to laugh in his company or to be uplifted. I used to think of fallen angels as people who had a bad start and made the best of their circumstances when they came to their senses. With James and with the ferry man, something else is coming to me. Their soul's code, perhaps, determined their terrible beginning in order to prepare them for the work of altruism. To be able to operate from a place of non-judgement on a mother who has left her children alone for days on end takes not only training but experience of what you will do when you are out of control. You will do anything. James was capable of anything. But it didn't stop those who loved him from trying to reach him:

'There was knock on the door one day. It was this fabulous-looking woman who pushed my sleeves up and started shouting. I didn't recognise her, then realised it was Julie. She had never looked as well when she was with me.'

She was there because of a chance meeting he had with someone from his hometown. A one in a million chance in 1970s London.

'I met this chap on Earl's Court Road. I remember saying to him to come round, not realising the state I was in or the state of the place. The room was used for hustling and using. There were towels all over the place, blood, rubbish. I was at the end of my tether and dirty myself. He went home and told Julie what I was living like and where I was.

'She was savvy about London so came over and started looking for me and found me. I just walked out the door and left Louise behind and came home on a ferry with Julie. A priest friend of hers met us off the ferry. I took a fit and ended up in St Michael's Hospital in Dun Laoghaire. It was 1979 and I'd never lived. I tried to break the window because I couldn't breathe. I had been trying to come off intravenous drugs by taking loads of barbiturates.

'The doctor told me if I stayed the night he would give me a shot. I put my arm up like a child getting a lollipop. They took me to Jervis Street to detox the next day but they were full up. I came home, to Julie's. I was home with her a week. A welfare cheque came in for her and the kids and it vanished, so she called a social worker and got her to come round while she told me, "I made a mistake. I should never have taken you back. You have to go." The social worker took me down to my mother's.

'I was a twenty-eight-year-old man with someone holding my hand. My mother opened the door and her expression said it all: He's mad. But I'll take him in. The social worker said they were trying to get me into a hostel in the neighbouring town.'

During this time, James's mother sat down with him and told him her own story. It was the beginning of his realisation that everyone has dark times and a sense of being unworthy, even the woman he respected most in the world:

'She told me this, one day, out of the blue. My mother had fallen in love with a man in her early twenties and had a child by him. My eldest brother, Michael, was illegitimate. This was in the 1930s. She came from a strict farm upbringing, was kept out of school to be the workhorse on the homestead. Her father said, "We can't be harbouring a sinner." They wouldn't let her sit down. They packed a bag for her and put it outside the door.

'It was the saddest thing I ever heard in my life. She hitched a lift into the nearest town and got a job in a big pub and grocery as a dogsbody. In those days everybody gave up illegitimate babies. My mother refused. The place where she worked was good to her and had room for her but not for her baby. So she paid a woman to mind the child all week and she got to see him on a Sunday. Her work during the week involved minding other children but she only got to see her own for a day at a time.

'By the time Michael was four she had met my father. They had seven children. One was born dead but the other who died was strangled by reins in the pram. My father was away working in England at the time. Her way of coping was to get down on her knees and pray for help. She was grieving and terrified that other people would think she was a killer or a terrible mother. She had to do it all on her own. I think she passed on her strength to us.

'The stigma of what had happened had controlled her life.'

Clearly she saw something in James she could answer with her own story. Why she chose to tell James, he doesn't know or commit to but knows the effect hearing it had on him.

'They didn't know about the abuse, or how disturbed I was. Having my mother speak to me the way she did helped me. I had always been the black sheep in the family. Even though they didn't disown me they didn't want to see me coming. With good reason.'

James had reached the bottom. He was in his mother's two-bedroom terrace, where he had scrubbed himself clean in the tin

bath after every abusive episode with his neighbours. Now he
was being tended for infected wounds by strangers, who involved
themselves in his story, hoping to help him, as his mother had done
by involving him in hers:

'My arms and thighs were covered in abscesses. The social worker
who had brought me to my mother was a knight in shining armour.
She got in touch with a nurse, who had a brother die from a heroin
overdose, who came down every evening to put poultices on my
arms and legs. I was afraid to go to doctors.

'They got me into a treatment centre and apart from dealing
with the physical addictions they introduced me to Narcotics
Anonymous. It was the single biggest thing that ever happened
to me. To sit with people like me. I heard stories that were like my
own, different from my own and worse than my own. But we all had
one thing in common. We had found a chemical solution. We used
chemicals to block pain and really they made it worse.

'Since October 1979 I haven't used drugs or taken a drink.'

He began to find a solution that was life-based and accepting that
even in his loneliest times, he had never been left alone. Something,
he won't put a name on what, was protecting him, even in the
hustling, the street life, the bloodied towels and dirty body. He always
had a sense of something bigger than humanity; it encouraged him
not to ignore lives more ordinary but to observe his own and the gap
between them. The first angel, for James, was himself; the second a
hometown neighbour who was walking along the right London road
at the right time and whom in a moment of madness he invited into
his real condition; then his wife, who loved him and followed him
through his life, then his mother, who gave him her own painful past,
when she knew he felt he was beyond saving; then a social worker,
who saw more than the disgraces, who saw the heart and soul,
pulsing underneath the lost skin; then a nurse, who took time out of
her own private life to care for his infected limbs and broken body,
because of the brother she had lost.

'The number of people who came in at that time. I had tried to
detox before, but without that kind of support.'

So many angels. Needed angels. He was on the street. Frozen out of existence but loved. Love drew him back in. Julie's love, mother love. The love of strangers. No one believed the stories. But no one gave up on him. The worst thing about addiction is that the people you love will always love the sinner and not the sin. They allow you to do horrendous things, because they have seen something you have given up on yourself. Or in James's case didn't know was there. They have glimpsed your soul. You are more than your acts.

The Dalai Lama's quote, on being open to the path of synchronicity, released from expectations, applies here. James's only expectation was that he would die soon. Then, one after the other, a relay of people came to his assistance, passing the baton, unaware they were all sharing a role in his recovery.

To understand why they involved themselves, you have only to meet him. His life force is visible even to an occasional visitor like me. The part of him that continued, that hadn't shut down on possibility, was about to spill upwards like an oil strike. In the twelve-step programme he came to know a God he had always been open to but hadn't been able to find. His interpretation of God is loose, a beautiful crochet of thoughts and coincidences rather than a dense knit:

'The programme leaves it open to interpretation, but you do refer to a Higher Power, because you are not able to beat this on your own. The great thing for me is that it's all suggested, it's not commandments. It's a spiritual programme. Atheists aren't excluded, no one is. I like that.

'Step One: You accept unmanageability and powerless. Step Two: You realise that you're nuts because nobody in the world would do the things you do. Step Three: You hand your will over to a higher power every day, or God, if you choose to call him that.' I hear the echo of Bernadette in this statement. It makes perfect sense. In the human experience, we need help from something beyond us.

'Step Four: You go in and look at your past. Look at the stuff I spoke about earlier. Abuse and so on. Filter through it, section it out and talk to someone about it. Look at the relevant details. I went to loads of issues in my life, separately, to move on from them. Things that happened, I began see how they were dictating my life to me now. The fourth step is an archaeological dig.' In forgiving others he learned to forgive himself, by seeing not only what he was but what he had been before the abuse changed him and set him apart from his own hopes:

'That was a big thing for me, setting me on the road to redemption. I was looking for it really, just wanted redemption. I never wanted to do the things I did, never ever.

'I saw I was an okay kid. I had become a scumbag. It's a term that a lot of people don't like to use but actually I had become one. To go and score drugs, I once left my child with a babysitter for three days. No one knew where I was. I was not a nice person. I made huge amends to all the people I hurt. But it began with me. The first person you do that to is yourself. I had become a self-fulfilling prophecy because I believed I was dirty from ten.'

What does redemption physically mean to James?

'I am clean. I am free. I am gay. I am okay with who I am. Talking to Julie about being gay, that wasn't hard. She met me in a gay bar and battered a lesbian to save me. We were Romeo and Juliet not! She took an overdose to stop me from taking one. When we were running from the police she got me arrested because she fell into a dustbin. I didn't leave her behind! I was noble! I pulled her out of it. She then went on to pull me out of life's dustbin. If it wasn't for her I'd have died in 1979 or 1980.'

Redemption has all been about acceptance, ultimately, and happiness. The acceptances and atonements continue more than three decades later:

'It took me a long time to truly accept my sexuality. I remember Julie and I, we were split up, going to a party as friends. A friend of mine, a very out gay man, got up and kissed me on the lips. I wanted to fucking deck him. Everybody at the party knew I was gay. Julie and I knew I was gay. But there had been no open display from me.

'I had to go home, sit down and think about why that had happened. My level of acceptance wasn't complete. It's been a bit harder but there's nothing you cannot do once you accept yourself and get on with it.'

What are the stages of self-acceptance?

'There's lots of different levels but one thing in all the stages: truth. I would say to you today am I sincere and truthful? Yes. Am I a thief and a liar? Yes. I think that's true of everybody. I work as a counsellor in a treatment centre. Once we acknowledge ourselves for who we are we can deal with the flaws in others. Everyone has grey areas. If I can accept myself fully, it makes it easier for me to look at you. If you've come to me for help and I can accept any of the actions you tell me you've carried out, hopefully you'll get the message and won't continue harming yourself, instead of judging yourself for your own actions. Addicts hate themselves. Someone needs to love them.'

Also some of the things you find hardest to accept are the things that make you unique:

'I see my sexuality today as a gift I was given. I didn't for a long time but when I stopped and thought about it, all my life I was able to understand the things that were going on with people, even horrible, bleak people and murderers up for killing. I was able to see the tragedy of it, not condoning it, but see the tragedy of the wasted lives, both theirs and the people they killed. That is a gift other people don't have.

'It's just spiritual connection I get with people. Can't put a name on it or define it completely.'

James turned his life around and gave to others what had been given to him:

'I met a man after Julie: Stephen. I lived with him for eleven years. He had the virus, HIV, and he developed AIDS and died. I nursed him. He and Julie were great friends. My kids loved him. I escaped getting the virus but I had Hep-C, little did I know. Stephen, by the time he got really sick, couldn't get up the stairs. I was on Interferon treatment for the hepatitis and I started to build the downstairs extension for him. People told me the Interferon would drive me crazy. I said I'd drive it crazy and started to put on extensions to my house. That's where all my crazy went, into extra rooms. I've had my children all living with me. They love me and I love them. I never told them about Stephen, specifically, but they learned it eventually and they loved him so much too.'

As well as putting up extensions he realised his condition was not going to allow him to work as a decorator forever. For years he had been volunteering to work with people in the prison system and on the street.

'I went back to school and college and I got a diploma in what I'd lived. Now I do it and get paid for it, something I would do for nothing.'

His particular interest is in working with those no one thinks will make it. Who've been in and out of treatment centres.

'We can take some people from prison and help them to get involved in life again. If they get out without doing that work, they go straight on to the street and get stoned. The chap I helped recently was in his mid-thirties and had spent half of his life incarcerated. I said to the judge: "The longest he has been clean is with our organisation." He had to believe he would recover. Recovery is an exercise in belief and faith. Your addiction tells you that you are useless. We get people to see that sin is only a flaw. Everyone has flaws. I come from despair. I come from a place where I never was going to have a life. Every morning I got up, I thought: I am going to die. It's going to be easy. Then Julie came back into my life and upset everything.'

His message to those he works with is simple:

'Fear, make it a friend, it's a good thing, there to warn you not to put your hand in the fire, but we have demonised it. Make it a friend. Being clean means facing up to what you've done. That's where the fear comes in. But you're not a bad person if you've done bad things. You're not evil. It's a day programme for street people, prisoners, for serious junkies. We take people who find it difficult in other places.'

The silence round the statement says how much he encounters on a daily basis. Does he believe evil exists?

'I have met people who have done evil things but they're not evil. I'm working with a man at the moment who was behind several murders. If he didn't pull the trigger he was behind the decision to. He was full of fear that people were trying to kill him so he retaliated before they could.

'Another girl who I work with has been made to participate in acts you don't want to know about. Every day she gets up, she's going to her own funeral. I try to tell her it isn't her. It's the people who did it to her. Paedophiles are the only ones I have ever met who were truly evil. If you have been abused you go for treatment so you don't abuse yourself when you get older. But there are people who have had the treatment who still talk about enjoyment. That's another level. That's evil. I tell them straight out.

'I point out too that addiction is a demon. I will say or do anything to drive it away, out of the person. They hate me for it some of the time. I know their despair.

'I've got a gift being able to listen and hear it as it is. Not as I'd like it to be. Not as it should be. As it is. I believe in love. I've seen it change the most awful lives. I couldn't have handled what happened in the second part of my life without the first part of my life.'

Spiritually James likes a little bit of everything:

'Sometimes I am envious of people who have Catholicism. A notion goes through my head to go back to the church. But they don't agree with me or the person I am. I try to be as fair and as honest as I can, so it would seem hypocritical to return.'

You can see that after all he went through to be who he is, it's not possible to deny it. It was this irrepressibility that got him through his lover's death and his own transplant:

'When Stephen died I did what my mother did. I got up and got on with it. But I had cirrhosis and my chances of getting liver cancer were increased. Then I got it. I had to have a transplant. I used to go to the gym and trained out of vanity. Now I do it to save my life.

'Four and a half years ago I was transplanted. It was the perfect match. It was an angel who had this liver. It was never used, I'm telling you. I've been taking her places she has never been to, doing things she's never done!

'They don't normally transplant livers from donors over the age of forty, because they usually stiffen up. But this one was perfect. It was extraordinary. A woman in her middle fifties who never drank or smoked in her life. I say I can't stop crossing my legs since I got it, getting very twee. There's no notable difference in me, other than this liver works, thank God.'

A feather floats down on him. I point to it and raise my eyebrow.

'I don't see anything significant in that. It's from a pigeon's arse. Full of bacteria. You're trying to kill me!'

By the time I stop laughing there are tears rolling down my face. Throughout his story he has kept me in stitches. Describing the horrors, he speaks with equanimity and a lack of aggression that comes from true peace and confidence.

Where does spirituality rest most comfortably for James? Where has his journey brought him? A return to innocence:

'I went back to being the child I was. Sitting on my mother's knee. She was combing my hair, dipping the comb in Loxene, for the curls. Happy.

'The stuff I have in my life today! I remember my eldest daughter was in treatment for addiction. My partner had AIDS. I hadn't yet gone on Interferon for the hepatitis. I was out in a house in Blackrock painting and put down the brush for a moment, realised how happy I was. Really happy. I burst out laughing and told myself, 'You can't tell anyone you're this happy. You're a bleeding house painter.' But I just felt this great feeling inside, this childlike feeling. I listen to sad stories all the time, in work, but I get a wonderful feeling that washes me clean. I can't name it or anything, I feel silly talking about it, but I just get these wonderful moments, still.'

His spirit was one of the reasons he survived his transplant and made an incredible recovery initially, but the drive in him drove him too quickly:

'My transplant went fine. I was out of intensive care within an hour. Moving my arms, saying: "Let me out of here. I want to fly." Back to the gym in seven weeks, back to work in eight weeks. I was doing a paint job for a friend in the evening and asked him: "What do you think of this?" When I showed him the wound he told me to get off the ladder and down to the hospital.

'They wanted to take me in immediately, but I had to go back out and take my car home and get the bus back into town.' Only James would think about being clamped at this time.

They admitted him and began to treat him for serious infection:

'Sins of the past, my veins die very quick. I had abscesses, poultices, just like the early days of my recovery. After eight days of this, I had a look in the mirror. I have a great denial mechanism, I can see my eyes and nothing else. But I had lost two stone in a few days. I caught a glimpse of myself, scars and everything, and thought, "I cannot do this, I haven't got anything left in me."

He remembered the poultices brought by the nursing angel; he thought of his early days detoxing:

'I used to get down on my knees at the side of the bed and pray. So I got down, again, at the side of the bed and said, "To whatever the fuck is out there, please, I need help."'

Hospital is a cage for him.

'They let me out the very next day with canisters of drugs. I never looked back. I've decided to take part in the Olympics for transplants and people on dialysis. The European Championships are coming to Ireland. I'm motivated now to take part in the games when they come to Ireland this year. I'm training every day.

'The only thing I don't wish to take part in is the fecking table tennis. I hate it. If I'd ever gone to prison, as I should have done, I'd have ended up being good at that. Anyone I work with out of prison is great at it. Ping pong, it goes on too long. Nothing small or sedate for me. I love the big things.

'Part of the thing for me, with my faith, is sitting down, talking to God, looking for answers. I couldn't meditate. I am ADD I think. But I can sit down on my own now. It comes more naturally. I am fifty-eight now. I still love training and exerting myself.

'When I am training I am talking to God. I get the answer when I pray. Usually to change things ever so slightly or leave things alone. Because I am a real fixer.'

Who has he become, on his angel journey?

'Contradictory. I am not that simple. I am complicated. I feel deeply, understand things beyond my own capabilities. Having said that, I am very practical, no nonsense.

'I remember in my early recovery a man used to come to tell us parables from the Bible. I was finding all the truth hard going, all the sharing. I just wondered if I could ever make it. In the group session he told the story of Mary Magdalene and I got it, the love thing. I started to fall asleep and one of the group said, "Look, James is asleep." All this man said was, "Leave him. He's fine." I liked him for that.

'That's redemption for anyone that wants it, it's there. No matter what you have done.'

As I leave his house I make him a promise, to bring him a book called *Simple Abundance*, which helped me to establish physical order in my home. But he's brought me something far more. I know now that my close friend, who died, is beavering away on this book beside me. That there are good people, right now, lying in doorways, who deserve an angel, to help them take their first steps on Redemption Street.

7

REDEMPTION STREET

I am sensitive to emotions and feel a lot of what's going on; from years ago this has been the way. Now I am aware of this I try to let it go through me and not hold on to the feeling. When there are moments like yesterday and today, with my mother, it all comes rushing back. I feel angry with her for being like that and always did. It was not nice coming home from school not knowing if there was going to be silence in the house.

I wished for a normal childhood with fun and laughter and friends over to play and hang out with; instead I got told, 'No,' that they couldn't come for some unknown reason. Anyway all this is being released from within and I need to be gentle with it. I hope there is understanding from the people in my family who are part of this and for once they will listen. I just want to live my normal life and feel happy within my heart, soul and spirit and to be free of the past hurt and bottled-up emotion. To release the memories that hold me back.

I have a sense of a higher frequency, vibration, happening all around and sometimes I am visual with higher energy and what I believe to be entities and more evolved beings of light floating around and shifting focus quickly. This is reassuring to me. I walk the right path and I need no drug or other negative influence to create a false reality and to keep me stuck in the past surrounded and driven by ego. Come forth to what is really real and so important in my life; natural living and creation is amazing and bright, surrounded by the beings of light, protecting me, keeping Eoin safe each step of the journey. Every day is a miracle delivered to us from above with love and lessons. Fairies are here.

Eoin, 2010

How does a man cry? Get up and get on with it, James's mother said. She was taught to do the same. The advice works. But what happens to all the feelings men have? The worst thing we have done to our men is to deprive them of visible tears. Some men find the answer in a pint glass, or in passion, or in drugs. Then they find their way back to the uncried tears. They claim them and, just like James, the life force that should have gone with them returns. You cannot keep a good man down.

There are lot of people living on Redemption Street. Here are two men, at opposite ends of the same story. Eoin is new to the street, Peter an old hand. When I first see Eoin again, I am in the place where I go to find the spirit of my life. I call them the happy woods. In the woods my dog spots him and I tense up because she always barks at men on their own. Her sight is not good and her trust of men isn't either. So I'm surprised when she walks up to him and he pats her head as if he's known her all her life. She stands by him and I catch up, relieved not have to explain her fears.

Then I see it's Eoin. He has been walking the road less travelled for the past four years. Both of us belonged to the same meditation circle and he was someone I identified as being intensely gentle and sincere. There's a tallness about him that comes from more than his height. Eoin works with the broken and sees their vulnerability and possibility. I know, like myself, he's a no house person. Like myself he has taken root here, close to the Blackstairs Mountains, because it's a place you can be free at any given moment. And the woods are happy. There's a spirit to this side of hill and what grows on it that hasn't been taken by a chainsaw and a logging quota.

We haven't seen each other in two years. I tell him about the journey and he says that he comes here to watch two hawks. He lies down in the woodland close to their nest and watches them circle overhead. He also comes here to meet the spirit of his life, walking here daily at a different time from me.

'I love the woods. Robin Hood was my hero as a boy and still is. Life takes us on journeys every day.'

We walk together and he agrees he will drop over some of his writing to me on the subject of the things he has seen and felt, on the places he has been. The previous extract is a small fraction of his thoughts, his written tears.

How has he made his way?

'Knowingly, my spirit journey began in Australia a few years ago but it was always going on inside me. Where has it taken me? Through drugs and too much of them, I was in a bad place: a lot of the visions I had weren't healthy. I talked to one of the girls I was working with on the farm, who practised Reiki, and she did an absent healing on me that night. She wrote down some of the things that came to her and gave it to me to read the next morning. It had so much about my past that fitted that I wanted to know more.

'I was very skint then, but money came and money was there for me to do a Reiki course.

'I remember well the first time I got a visual sense of my soul's journey. It was at the course, out on a balcony watching the clouds move over a beautiful sky. I saw small balls of light flying around me. I never looked into them. I just trusted they were there. Seeing those beautiful little lights opened my eyes up to a lot of things. I felt myself moving towards something I didn't understand.

'My trust started to build. Then I went back to London and I slipped into some old ways. I wasn't in touch with good friends and wasn't practising Reiki. The drugs took over again. But I knew in my heart I was on the wrong path and doing the wrong things. I was lost again and I needed to find my way. But it took a few years. People came into my life in the middle of it all. I always knew I would get back to the right space and place. Two years ago I started on a course and did an essay on depression. It triggered something in me. It wasn't right. My body was rejecting the drugs. I felt I was being taken to a lower place and vibration. I gave up smoking dope and cut right down on alcohol. It's been tough, shit, and the past has come up to be cleared.

'Good people and unseen things are there to support me. I have spiritual guides. I can't see them but I know they are there. It's trusting that you have support. A father-figure was missing from my life for a long time and I know that my grandfather, who has passed, is with me. Older relations who have passed are with me. I didn't get upset at their funeral because I knew that they were still with me and I had another good spirit looking out for me.'

For Eoin nature offers its protections:

'If you've love in your heart, you share it with everyone. It starts within you. It's just a knowing. They're there at the lowest times in my life. There might not be anything going on spiritually, but you have the support. A feather will drop in front of you. A hawk circles overhead. I love the woods; sometimes they feel more like home than home.

'I understand my past a lot more, seeing the triggers in it. I used to walk in the woods and asked the keeper of the forest to guide and protect me. I knew the hawk was there for me, to guide.'

He's working now with the child and young adult he was:

'I go as far as bringing in the symbols to the people who are using the head shops so that they can be kept safe. Young people think because the stuff is legal it's safe. They want to rebel but want to rebel within safe limits.'

He gives me a part of his journal to read, called 'Stories Released', to explain the reasons behinds his addictions. Being a quiet man, not prone to verbosity, the written word is how he best communicates. He describes how much he loves the woods and I am drawn in, from the first words, to his story:

'I love the way life is. The power of oneness and the colour of the wind. As I write, each word becomes a history, memories race and the story lengthens. Sometimes the learning happens with the results following later. Conflict doesn't serve me any more.'

Eoin's creativity, blocked by the drug heaven, is resurfacing. Peter's fingerprints are on the reclamations of many a creative act and many a creative human being, myself included. He is a writer, theatre director, playwright, screenwriter, film director and gifted public speaker. His story is one of recovery from addiction and self-loathing.

Everyone can find their way to Redemption Street if they hang on long enough and gather enough belief. People like Peter appear, long-time residents. He mentors a lot of lost souls in their recoveries from missed chances and spoiled opportunities. He is calm in his commentary and old in his thinking. He doesn't involve himself in your crisis but he understands how crises begin and develop and appreciates when they end.

He is writing and directing all over the place, in his own words: 'Doing the right thing at the right time.' I'm grateful for his honesties. For knowing him. Real friends enrich your life.

Peter was one of the persuasions that I should come out of mourning. If my darkness and behaviours were harsh, Peter went to an altogether darker place. The bottom of a bottle. We spoke to each other rarely but his sentences and his examples were like torches. He spoke about loss. The loss of his writing way. The depth to which he had to sink in order to reach a surface. A near-fatal accident, by drowning, in 2004, gave him his chance to review all he was and all he had become.

'We grew up embarrassed by our spirituality. In the old days our teachers and priests got it so wrong with the punishing God. We were primed to reject it. When the shit hit the fan with the church, old beliefs fell away and people were left with nothing to fall back on. This hell they invented, this purgatory where unbaptised children were placed for twenty-five years. As Joyce said, he wanted no part or place with a father in heaven that put them there.'

Being taught to think yourself impure, being punished in itself, wouldn't have led Peter to a renunciation of the spiritual. The death of his brother Frankie, when Frankie was ten and Peter fifteen years old, in 1967, changed the course of his life and the nature of his belief:

'I blamed myself for his death. When he was diagnosed with a brain tumour I got down on my knees and prayed that my family would be spared the heartache. When he was operated on I prayed. I believed if I prayed hard enough and strong enough God would save Frankie. God didn't.

'I left that period of my life so angry. I thought, "Fuck you." But I never lost belief.'

He lost neither God nor anger:

'Around this time my drinking started.'

Peter describes himself as the funny drunk, the one who got into trouble with his drinking. The one friends had amusing stories about the next day. He was on the whiskey straight away while others were drinking pints. He was a spirit man:

'I heard somebody describing drinking as a low-level search for God. That was what it was for me. The God I lost faith in when Frankie died. What did this mean? I carried this wound, nursed all these feelings in relation to my belief in the higher power. My relationship with God was chaos, a finger pointing, an "you owe me" relationship. "If you get me through this drunken phase, if you heal this wound in my marriage, if you this, if you that." It went on and on. Then it had to stop. The drinking just didn't work any more.

'People didn't know what was going on. I wasn't the kind who lost my house, job and car. My sister says she never saw me as an out-of-control drunk. But she wasn't inside my head. It was crazy in there. I started to have panic attacks. That was the final thing. When I couldn't travel on the subway in New York, when I couldn't go to parties because the number of people overwhelmed me, I knew it had to be time.'

He describes his sobriety as a journey. The first place it took him to was a rekindling of the trust he had lost in spirit:

'The first step in stopping drinking was rediscovering something that had been dead inside me for a long time. One of the first things to happen was the reconnection with spirit. Leaving down the glass and the drugs brought me back to a Peter I had forgotten was there: a soft person, a kind person, a person worth knowing. I really liked this part of myself. It was a good time, this first chance to be aware of myself and be open to what was coming for me.'

Previously he had been closed and frightened. He had a hard job liking himself. The panic attacks, although hard to experience and worse to anticipate, were part of his message: that something more was waiting for him. There were other messages:

'I don't believe there are coincidences. I met people from then on in my journey because I was ready to meet them. I was a pupil ready to meet teachers.'

One of the angels in his early walk was a woman who was terminally ill with cancer.

'She was at a meeting in the US that I attended. She wasn't going to live long and she was okay with that. She was facing annihilation and she was fearless, happy, content and embracing. This was the Christian message my early education didn't give me.' In sharing her last weeks, when they became close friends, Peter learned two things, one about Frankie and how to come to terms with his early death, the other in relation to himself:

'She taught me how to die. She taught me that dying is okay. Even though she had so little time she wasn't going to drink because she wanted to be properly in all of her last moments. I came to terms with my own mortality through seeing how she dealt with hers. Up until then I was scared to die because of my experience of how Frankie died.'

The 'secret' grief that Martha talks of in the chapter 'All My Relations' was Peter's grief. His family never spoke about Frankie's death or Frankie. It wasn't that Frankie was forgotten: he was remembered in every given day but not openly, because of the pain Peter's parents felt. Peter tried on two occasions to acknowledge it and his mother in particular resisted it:

'We weren't given the opportunity to cry the tears and share the grief. It was a question of: "Don't you get in the way of my grief. This is mine. It belongs to me." So we suffered on our own.'

This is the very antithesis of how Kathy's family cope with her son Kevin's drowning in 'The Blue Love'. They speak of Kevin every day and his picture is everywhere. A similar situation is found with Catherine and her family in 'Coming Alive'. They acknowledge the presence of their lost baby, Jessica, whose spirit is found in every moment in their new and daily lives.

A spiritual awareness and sharing of the mortal experience, those we lose too early in it, reminds us we are going to live, love and lose; this is a key to coping with death. Peter, whose whole life is based on expression, was not given this chance but created it for himself in his work:

'The impact on my writing and on my performance was huge. All of it was working out that conundrum: "How do you continue to believe in the face of something so traumatic?"'

To live on Redemption Street you have to deal with the shit. You have to deal with the betrayals and denials, especially your own. You have to acknowledge, publicly and privately, that you have been caged. Then, it seems, the key is put into your hands.

Eighteen months into Peter's angel journey, he was ready to deal with his bereavement – years after it had happened:

'I was in Austin, Texas, when I was thirteen months sober, to direct a play for a theatre run by a friend of mine. A great man of the theatre, an older man than me. I have always made very strong friendships with older men. It's a father thing. He was a mentor to me.

'I went to a twelve-step meeting and heard a man talking about his childhood and his relationship with a woman which his parents broke up. In sobriety he made contact with her to ask forgiveness. The break-up of the relationship made him lose more than her: he lost her parents who were better than his own to him. On the way to meet her, in person, he had a crash and ended up in hospital. She came to see him there.

'It was such a story of love, forgiveness and redemption that I went back to the Green Room of the theatre full of my own childhood, full of Frankie, my brother. I was convulsed with pent-up grief and loss, it came welling back up in me and I found myself on my hands and knees, praying. I realised there was a solution and that it was all about the spirit inside me.

I cried for three days. The way they talk about rays of light coming down, it was that sensation. Only it was inside me. I knew I was being transformed by the spirit infusing me. Like God's holy spirit helping me to become whole again. I knew then there was a higher power who forgave me because I could forgive myself. In learning to forgive myself I sensed the presence of this awesome being who thought only good of me. I had a huge spiritual awakening, finding a spirit I had lost thirty years earlier. I needed almost to become an alcoholic in order to find this road. The drinking had been for a reason. It wasn't purposeless. I tell you, I just grabbed that knowledge with both hands.

'I gave it a chance and I've been sober since. I've fallen by the wayside and made terrible mistakes in other areas along the way.

We're duty-bound to pass on the message. I do it to the best of my ability.'

Peter came away with one of the big lessons. Successes are transitory. Acclaim and applause passes. Achievements are finite. How kind you are is all that really matters and all you can really be remembered for:

'It's really about how I live my life. My values, my basics, are to deal with what is crazy on any given day by not drinking, not hurting anyone. I might have a bad day but not drinking is my foundation, my cornerstone. It's how I hold faith and belief in myself. I have a deep belief in a higher power. You couldn't come through a twelve-step recovery programme, as I have, without that. Although I know people who do, I think you short-change yourself. None of us is perfect, none of us can carry all the pain ourselves.

'The key for me was the concept of a loving God, as opposed to a punitive one. In sobriety I found that loving God, I'd always known he was there but I didn't trust. And I found out lots about myself, my weakness. I have sides of myself that I would be embarrassed to reveal, to you or to anybody. It's in our sinning we find humanity. The awful cliché is a true one – the whole thing is about self-forgiveness.

'My life journey has been about celebrating my deficiencies rather than punishing myself for them. I did the latter for a long time. Alcoholic drinking is all part of that process. It's hard to be an alcoholic, to live that lifestyle, because at the core you know that it's not working, yet you persist with failure. You need a lot of self-will for that.'

Finding a way of not being that person is really difficult. But no harder than living with a low-level search for God, when you want a higher one:

'Being a practising alcoholic is so demeaning, so dispiriting. It kills the spirit. In a way sobriety is about rekindling spirit. Finding the fun and the humour and lightness in life again. From early on, the drinking turned me into somebody I didn't like. I became moody, cantankerous, I could be difficult when I was drunk – particularly inside the four walls of my own house. I took other drugs along the way. But funnily enough I always cut them out because they got in the way of my drinking.

'Writing and directing, drinking is part of it, late nights after the show, stress, incredibly highs and lows, adrenaline, nerves. Something in my head said, "Give up and see what happens."

'I ended up having a series of panic attacks that floored me. I could be on a train or bus, in the middle of the day. My heart would start pounding, I'd have to get somewhere safe. All those awful feelings took over my life.

'On 15 August 1989 I had a serious episode in Edinburgh. I knew that was the end of the familiar road and I was off on the one Scott Peck, quoting Robert Frost, calls "less travelled by". I met many people along the way who didn't have the courage to leave drink behind and ended up killing themselves. They were always people who were smart, clever. Their intellect got in the way of their recovery because they thought they could outsmart drink. You can't if it's got you. I have learned more about myself through the process of putting down the drink than through anything else.

'When I get interested in something I tend to obsess and that obsession is about trying to stop myself feeling. I use the interest as a way of switching off from things I should be doing, like looking at emotions. I can use gambling, the horses. I could easily have a problem in that direction if I didn't watch myself.

'I've had a huge problem with intimacy all my life. To me intimacy meant that I loved my little brother and he died when he was ten and I was fifteen. I've always a huge problem about getting too close to people or letting people get too close to me. My experience of it was that they could disappear on you. So don't depend on that one.

'I have done things I am deeply ashamed of. But I have always found my way back. That's the spirit of my life.'

The common bond of these men, who are strangers to each other, is that they lost the power of expression in childhood: James through abuse, Peter through bereavement and Eoin through a terrible silence and isolation. All of them chose annihilation to drive feeling away; all of them found their way back through powerful

messages; all of them intend to remain rooted in redemption and live
its rewards.

All that was lost, back in the day, has been reclaimed. There is no
innocence but there is the sympathy they now show for themselves.
These men had all the feeling and none of the opportunity to express
it as children. Our society's demands and concerns overrode their
natural sensitivities. The very quality that gives these men their
strength in grown lives was deprecated. Eoin has begun the journey
Peter and James began, also in their mid-thirties. They are free to cry.
This is an inheritance they gave to themselves.

Some people are born with an inheritance they didn't want.
Catherine is one of them. She has used her inheritance to help
recover the bodies of lost souls who didn't make it to Redemption
Street. 'Talking to the Dead' is her story.

8

The Blue Love

Crossing over. From life to death. From womb to life. The journey is similar in physicality and in spirituality. One contributor saw her father in the room as she held her son in her arms for the first time. He had died during her labour and no one had told her.

What do you imagine death to be?

This is a question I've asked many interviewees, for many years. I wanted not just to know their view but to expand my own. Invariably the answers were about what comes next, rather than the process of dying.

Isabel is a world-famous writer but, more than this, a woman of spirit. She gave me the first indicator of the mystery, spirit and similarity of the birthing and dying experience in an interview long ago. Her daughter, Paula, aged twenty-seven, died in the same bed in which her granddaughter was born. She feels her daughter to be a soft presence around her.

'She fell sick suddenly. There were stages of terrible fear and great, irrational hope. I would have awful dreams…

'Breathing was the only thing she could do. Then I took her home and my job really started. We set up a small hospital on the first floor of our house. We really moved our family life there – we had the television set there; my grandchildren were born in the same room. Everything happened around Paula's bed. We were there with her twenty-four hours a day.

'It was a time when we slowly gave up on the idea that she would recover; we slowly accepted that she was going to die before anybody else in the family.

'She died on 6 December, exactly one year to the day after she had first fallen into the coma. It was a very peaceful night and we started to share stories about Paula with one another. By three o'clock in the morning she died. I do not remember it as anything awful. A few months later my granddaughter was born in the same room. And the moment of Nicole's birth was identical to the moment of Paula's death.

'I can only describe it as a sort of stillness. Struggle beforehand, then stillness. The struggle was being born for Nicole and leaving the body for Paula. There was some pain, it was messy. But it was also very mysterious. When Paula was leaving her body and for some time after she died, I had the clear sense that there was a spirit that was slowly leaving the body and going somewhere else.

'When my granddaughter was being born I had the sense that she was coming from a place that was not only the womb. She was coming from a spiritual place – when I pulled her out of the womb, still with the cord around her, my first question popped out: "Tell me how it is, before you forget."'

'Maybe it was because it was the same room and the same bed in which Paula had died but I felt that Nicole was coming from the same place that Paula had gone to. It was an overwhelming sense, a striking revelation of how this mystery of life works.

'Paula must have known this before she lapsed into a coma. I went to her apartment to collect her clothes. The clothes were gone. She had given them all away. I don't think she knew that she was going to die. But she knew what was important. She had been in a retreat for a few days just before she got sick. She was a Catholic. When she came back from that retreat she had the stomach pains. One of the things she said to me was, "Mother, I am looking for God and I cannot find Him anywhere."

'My reply to that was, "God can wait, right now you need a doctor." Now I remember the struggle and search and anxiety she spoke of. They were the last words she spoke to me, apart from, "I love you." They were her very last words.'

I never forgot Isabel's.

The death of Paula bears a striking similarity to the death of Kevin, in the preparations Isabel made, without knowing. Kevin is the son of Kathy, who was an MEP up until recently. But he had found the God Paula searched for so frantically. And his death was unexpected: there was no long goodbye. Still, his mother had been prepared in the stages Isabel describes by a synchronicity of event and a premonition.

Both women found peace in the knowledge of what they experienced with their children in the time immediately before their passing.

The bridge between their experiences is Moira, a woman who has nursed at both ends of life, a woman who has buried her own. A woman of life with a world of awareness of the spiritual nature of birth and death. I find, as she speaks to me, that she is a silver fire. A chalice of knowledge which she sees as elementary but in fact is the very essence, direct experience of the crossing-over from known to unknown, not just for her own but for strangers. For four decades she been accompanying those for whom it is time to live and time to die, these times when the material nature of life vanishes and the mystery takes over. But she was being made ready for her work, even as a child:

'My first experience of death was some time in the 1950s, when my mother brought me to the wake of a mother and baby who had died in childbirth. I remember the crowds, the piercing cold, the terrible sadness that surrounded everyone in that awful room, particularly the women. The only heat or life I felt was in the connection between my mother's hand and mine.

'I was troubled by the thought of that young mother and baby going down into the cold clay and the terrible permanence of death and even though I was learning in the great Catholic tradition of God, the Holy Spirit and life hereafter, I did not equate it in any way with the physical smothering of a young woman in a wooden box, her little dead baby placed in the coffin with her. I felt my mother's hand as she gripped mine tighter.

'I became a student nurse in 1970. We learned how to carry out procedures but I never remember being told about dying or death, apart from the practicals of washing the body, plugging orifices, tying toes together, tying a bandage around the chin at the correct tension so as not to leave a mark and attaching it to the bar of the bed-head to stop the jaw opening until rigor mortis set in.

'The body was left for an hour after death before 'laying out' and the windows opened to allow the soul to leave the body and the room. I carried out the practicalities without a problem, as I was always very biddable and had learned in the authoritarian system in which we worked. Our fears or emotions were something that should never surface as we were expected to show a professional front at all times. In hindsight I always felt a bit scared around death, as if some unseen part of that dead person, whom I didn't personally know, yet was now sharing the most intimate part of their life, lurked in the room somewhere above me, watching. I don't know if it was my fear of the unknown or a feeling of soul presence.

'A few days into my first experiences on the wards, when I reached one of the beds, a lady, I can't remember her name, just her beautiful face and smile, asked if I would help her out to the commode.

'I saw love in those eyes. No fear. I was a young eighteen-year-old. She had such a powerful, beautiful face, the look of a film star, I have no idea how old she was but she could have been anything over fifty. Anyone over forty was old to me. There was love in her face and in her eyes. The way she smiled at me, she was allowing me to be with her, to be part of this journey. She was loving me by letting me be with her, I remember.

'I can't describe her eyes with words, but I know I saw the same quality in my sister's when she was dying. There is a transparency in the colour of the eyes. A transparency. You can't use any other word for it. This experience is beyond words.

'This woman, she would have been the first of so many people whose last moments I shared. I never saw fear in those last moments. The nurse in me would put it down to medication but in the case of that woman she was not medicated. Her death was sudden.

Her head slumped forward. I was holding her with both my hands under her armpits and instantly, through my hands, could feel the life-force draining from her. I called out for assistance and proceeded to say an act of contrition in her ear. I remember the fervency of my prayer on her behalf and how uselessly out of control and unskilled I felt. I don't know why that memory has stayed so vividly with me for so long, when I have since been lucky enough to be with so many at the beginning and end of life.'

The next death that felt close to this in nature was her sister's, forty years later:

'The next time I saw the transparency was in my sister's eyes. She was drifting in and out of comas and came out of it for the last time on a Friday. Her eyes became a blue I remembered from the first death. The feeling of the blue is more real than the words I can use. I believe that was the time her spirit left her body. There were a few more days when the body kept functioning physically but the surge of that transparent light was prior to this.

'It was a blue that was full of love.'

The blue love is something Moira shares; her eyes have the piercing nature of stained glass. Something of what she has seen and done makes up their colouration. She has seen a different blue in the eyes of newborns, an older blue than the eyes at the point of death:

'I loved working in midwifery because we dealt in new life and, thankfully, rarely with death. No matter how dire the circumstances surrounding the birth, there was always something hopeful and life-sustaining about a new baby coming into the world. I sometimes wondered, often in the dead of night, working in nurseries, what "knowing" was behind the little piercing newborn eyes staring out at me and often felt that cold chill of being in the presence of something I didn't quite understand. All their eyes were blue, a different blue, a darker blue, maybe even an older blue.'

Her experience doesn't blunt her pain; if anything she knows all the ends and extremes of life:

'I have fought with life, with living and dying, caring, loving and losing and during those times have cried out for help, but when I stop crying and listen I get the sense of knowing that what I need is there, in and all around me in the eyes of people I love and meet.

'When my father died. I know he chose to die in my home, to have me there for his ending in this life. He died in his sleep. My first reaction was to open the window to free his spirit. I was conditioned to do that, yet I knew his spirit could transcend all windows and walls. I could feel his spirit all around me. Whenever I felt I needed his easy presence if I went into that room he was there. I believe butterflies are my sign that my departed loved ones are around me. When my sister died one swooped around her coffin all during the funeral mass and would turn up afterwards often when I was at my lowest. It helped me deal with grief at the time. And does still.

'Of course I doubt it but if I don't believe, what else do I have? A butterfly appeared last winter in the room my father died in and for a few days would flutter around when I felt or needed to feel his presence. Then it disappeared and with it the feeling of my father being in that room.

'I call on all my deceased family members from time to time and sometimes feel even closer to them than when they were alive. I've been with them all when they died. My mother and sister, I felt their spirits pass a couple of days before they took their final breaths.

'I wish I knew. I wish I understood. I don't! I see and I feel and sometimes I believe deeply and I survive and when I don't believe, I hurt. I am only human and from my experiences of life and death, know and believe there is continuity. In what form, I don't understand. I see the face and hands of God in my simple life – butterflies, babies, youth, the sick and elderly – and leave it to the people with genuine talents to put words on the simplest, most elusive part of lives, our being.'

I see Moira cover up her hands and ask her why. She finds them big and ugly, from the years of work and scrubbing that went into them. But they're beautiful prayer hands. They have cared for new life and going life and all the life in between.

Just like Moira, who has been both midwife and palliative care nurse, Kathy was given the realisation of how similar and spiritual the experiences of death and birth can be.

Kathy is a true friend, an *anam cara*. Our regard for each other overrides the differences in outlook. I am a refugee from hierarchical religion. She is a devout Catholic, as was her son Kevin, who drowned last year in an accident.

It's such a new grief.

She drives to see me, to share the synchronicity of events that led up to Kevin's drowning, a death she sees as tragic but not tragic for her son:

'That last physical journey he went on, before he went into the lake, all that day, it was as if he was responding to a call.'

We discuss the nature of messages. She has a convinced faith in angels. As my journey advances I think I have more faith in the angelic in people and synchronicities that indicate spiritual guidance for us. A friend of mine who is in her late eighties, who has worked with unsafe children all her life, can still say, 'We are all cared for.' I am more convinced of this. But I am not prepared to use the word 'angel' other than as symbolic term. Kathy's faith is direct and trusting; she believes she has a guardian:

'Angels are pure spirits; that is, they have no body. They live in the constant loving presence of God, whom they serve in many ways. My guardian angel is at the same time in eternal happiness and glory with God and dealing with me…what a contrast! It can't be easy!'

She's a tiny slip of a woman. Her calmness comes from a lot of cried tears and her unshakable faith:

'Often we're not listening for spiritual messages. This is when we stumble. But other times we are not meant to hear them. It was important that I be prepared for Kevin's death but it was equally important that he not be aware. He didn't anticipate things well. He got more and more nervous. In the weeks before he started any new thing it got bigger and bigger in his mind. Kevin couldn't have had advance warning but he was prepared.'

Instead of testing her faith, his drowning has brought it to a deeper sense. When Kevin went to the bottom of the lake, Kathy went to the bottom of her soul.

'I have learned in a new way that God is merciful. He was there before the death, he was there through it, he is there when I am walking through the house and it hits me that I am never seeing Kevin's face again. When he was due to come home from college, or when it was coming up to his birthday, I was helped. God is there. Grief. It's like a wall collapsing in on me. He eases me out from under it.'

By the time she's finished saying this, I am in tears. Kathy says she has no public tears left. She is helped, each day:

'It's just to be open to that all the time. I will never be able to get over how I was prepared for Kevin's death – how gentle it was, how absolutely exact it was and how the preparation was just what I needed, so I could understand. Otherwise I would not have been able to understand.

'It goes back to the very beginning. He was the only one of my babies who kept threatening to disappear before he was born. I had to go to hospital and have a lot of bed rest. It was my only pregnancy like that. Praying he would make it. He was baptised very shortly after he was born. He was an amazing, beautiful baby; of my nine he was one of the quietest. He didn't cry so I had to keep checking him. He had a lot of suffering so he was mature in himself. It gave him a lot to give to other people.

'He wound up having two hospitalisations and grommets for ear trouble. There's something about people who suffer or experience pain, if they incorporate it into their lives. He was often awake in the dark all night, holding himself in a certain position because of the pain but not calling out. His earaches disappeared but his headaches and migraine began.

'It had a deepening effect on him. He had huge empathy for people who have a hard time. He had never done well in school in Ireland but blossomed once he left Ireland. Then he got to go to his college, Southern Catholic College in America, which was more concerned about the kind of person you were than your grades. Kevin believed in Christ so much; he was devoted to the Eucharist.'

'The spiritual preparation he had done, a lot of us might reach at eighty or ninety.'

Kathy's immediate preparation for her son's death was losing her seat in the 2009 European election:

'Those weeks, in the summer, when I would have been back in Brussels, having been re-elected, I was home, with them all. Everybody in my family made sacrifices with me being an MEP. I got let off the hook to be with them. I see that now. I thank God every day for those three weeks when I was home and they were all there.

The lads were all building a shed together. I loved cooking, cleaning and gardening again. I fed them all up. I just loved doing honest work again.'

But Kathy is a person driven to more than domesticity. Her family knew that more than anyone. Another preparation came for her when one of her family, who works as an early childhood development expert, called her to share some information. She had come across the work of the hospice movement and was amazed to realise just as there are developmental stages to birth, so there are to death. Her thought was that Kathy should do some research on this correlation.

Every death accompanied by hospice staff is unique but there is a similar pattern of events. Just as midwives look at physical indicators of impending birth, so do palliative care nurses see indicators of impending death. Kathy found herself drawn further into the topic and began to learn lessons on leaving life and its spiritual dimensions:

'Just as children go through the stages, so do the dying. Each tiny thing leads to the next thing. Their work turned out to be very similar. It's something important to what we become, to completing us in death, just as it adds to us in early life.

'It's not only that it follows definite physical and emotional events: it's very spiritual. It's as if all your life has built you up to this time. Every experience in your life has brought you closer and closer, more in touch, every suffering, every childbirth; every event potentially could and should, if we are not resistant to it, bring us closer and closer to a sense of God, of spirit and our own souls.

'Hospice staff deal with physical pain but that's minor compared to the emotional, intellectual and spiritual pain that comes with this growth stage. When the child is born, they have to go through this squeezing and pulling to arrive. The same for the dying.

'Everyone gets this compulsion to confess. In an Irish hospice many people are raised Catholic and have a formula for release there, even if they haven't been to confession for thirty years. But many aren't Catholic and they still have to tell somebody, not just the story of their life, but the story of what they did. A woman calls for her cousin to come from the UK and as soon as she comes into the room, she tells her, "I cut the hair off your doll.'"

As the midwife guides life, the deathwife recognises the stages and responds to them:

'Another thing is saying goodbye. Even those who don't know they are dying say goodbye. They finish things off, complete things. At an unconscious level they know.

The last stage is this desire to go on a journey:

'Almost all terminally ill patients will call the nurse to book a ticket for them or make travel arrangements. The nurse knows they're not going anywhere, they often have drips and tubes inserted, but still will talk to them about arrangements and take them seriously and say they have made them.

'The hospice nurse goes with it all so the patient does not get agitated. They will pack a bag and leave it in the corner of the room so the patient relaxes. They are all going somewhere, they know, but they're not thinking in terms of where. All they have to do is wait now.'

A midwife finds the mother nesting. She thinks she is cleaning. But in fact she has this instinct. It won't matter what the charts say; the midwife will say the baby is going to be born soon. Similarly, after the desire to go on a journey, a hospice nurse will go to the nurses' station and say, 'We've had the conversation.' They will call the family because it will be within twenty-four hours, sometimes much sooner. For Kathy, gaining this knowledge, before Kevin's death, was providing her with insight:

'I remember looking at the research and being at ease. It took an incredible amount of fear away for me. I found this all reassuring. I had assumed you died; it just happened. But it's a whole process of development for the person. I remember thinking about that on and off for the rest of the summer.'

The next step in the family's preparation for Kevin's death was that his brothers and one sister got to spend a last weekend with him at Electric Picnic:

'They had this little crêpe van. It had taken a huge loss, with helping me to campaign doing the election and the wash-out weather. They pinned all their hopes on this festival. But it rained and rained. They really pulled together. If it had been less awful they wouldn't have been half as close.

'As I said, even people who don't know they are dying are saying goodbye. They finish things off, complete things at an unconscious level. Kevin and his brother, David, were due to go back to the States the next day, so I drove up to get them. I just wanted to spend time with them.

'I went down the wrong way in a one-way street in Cork and got stuck. I was hemmed in. It took me so long to get out of it. They were in hysterics at how crazy I was. We wound up laughing a lot. That was a huge interaction, after the tension was over. I was grateful for the mistake.'

The following day Kevin's brother Joady had to drive their van back from the festival, on the day of Kevin's departure, with his brother David, back to the States:

'"Don't let them go till I get there," he urged me. He had missed them going before. He saw them off four times a year and had just spent the whole weekend with them. We were sitting outside the airport and Kevin was worried that they would miss their flight. All of a sudden, just as I said, "You have to go," Joady came over the hill, running towards them. They jumped on one another. A few jokes. Off they went, with him saying, "I'll see you at Christmas." It was a few seconds. No one will forget them.'

The last thing Emma, his youngest sister, said to her brother was, "I love you. Big hug."'

Kevin died two and a half weeks after they went back to school. His mother began to feel a sense of premonition a week before it happened. And the signs mounted:

'That whole week before Kevin died, I knew one of my kids was going to die. I knew but I kept thinking of the two who were living at home. I was following them, hanging around them, in the workshop, watching them work the electric saw. I am not a fussy mother. I am laid back.

My son was putting up this big heavy shelf, he was hammering away. All I could do was watch the hammer go back and forth near his head. I kept thinking, "Is this how it's going to happen? Is that how he's going to go?"'

'Another night, the other son went out to work on his car, to run the battery, I told him every reason he shouldn't go out. I stood at the window watching, thinking this was the last time I would see him alive. I don't do that either. I usually have ten different things on. Then he came back twenty minutes later and I felt great.'

I know this to be true. I have spent time in Kathy's home, a bungalow in Ballinhassig with enough family to have a street parade. It's an infectious atmosphere, absorbing guests like water in a sponge. My two boys were babies when we last visited and her daughters took them away for the days we were there. It's down to her relaxed style and parenting policy – she rarely gives out to children and, in the words of her son Joady: 'Never apologised for our behaviour. We were being children.' Her sister Bridget died and she took in her seven also. There is not much she dreads. But the sense of dread grew.

'Every night that week I would wake, sit bolt upright, as if someone had splashed me with cold water. It was out of a very deep sleep, sensing, knowing someone was going to die. I would start to pray. I would worry and pray. I began to feel so much as if it was not just going to happen but that whoever it was wasn't ready. It just kept hitting me, I didn't think about it all the time but at night in particular I was in a cold sweat.

'I remember one night I had a bowl of ice cream and settled down with a book. I woke up that night, and said: "No more ice cream. Make a sacrifice." That was three nights before Kevin died. I knew that I was giving it up for my kids. I don't see God as somebody who punishes. I see us as people who choose God or don't choose. We choose ice cream, politics, cul de sacs.

'I remember praying myself back to sleep. I haven't had ice cream since.'

I feel a jolt at this. I had collected Kathy outside my children's school to take her to our home. We stopped off for ice cream. She smiles when I remind her.

'It was the nearest thing I ever had to an addiction. The night of Kevin's death, odd things happened. My attention was being drawn to different things. Earlier in the day I was in traffic. I usually listen to talk radio or the news. Just as I was switching a channel, I heard this haunting song, Susan Boyle singing "Wild Horses". I found myself listening to every word. It was about a young person dying. I wasn't thinking of death 24/7. The song was in my head all day, though, particularly the last line: "So let's do some living after we die."

'I went to ring Kevin that night, to ask his advice on something. I couldn't get the phone working. I left it on the bed, went to sleep. At five in the morning, Stephen, my son, came in and said, "Mom, there's a problem. They can't find Kevin."'

'I sat up and said, "That's because he's dead."'

Kevin had got into difficulties swimming across a man-made lake close to his college. Kathy, while she has no doubt that God prepared her for the terrible news, found it no less terrible:

'I remember immediately thinking, "Oh no." But also: "Thank God. He was the one who was ready. It's terrible. But he was ready." The last time I phoned was to tell him I had gone to the funeral of a man who had been in his class at school. I had just a few days before gone to the funeral of his classmate, who had also died swimming across a lake. He knew about it. He had been praying for J.P. There were only four boys in their class.

'We sat around stunned. We got through to David, who was also over there and he was distraught. He passed us over to the new president of the college. We were told the divers were searching the lake. Kevin had just been to confession.'

Again it seemed to be preparing. He was unusually determined to get it, not prepared to wait a day for when confession normally happened. His girlfriend even went looking for a priest for him and a friend, for this reason. Jessica's last time with Kevin was also meaningful. They were sitting in the chapel together, without words, in front of the Eucharist. For his confession, she found a new chaplain, by chance, who had just come to the college:

'He couldn't tell, of course, but he could say Kevin had had a very good confession. Just amazing, deep and true. He had been amazed at the depth Kevin reached.'

Twenty minutes later Kathy and two of her sons left the house

to catch a flight to Atlanta. Her daughter Brigid had phoned Dublin
airport and they were helped all the way on to the flight:

'When we arrived, we got word they had found Kevin's body.'

As the story unfolded over the week Kathy and her family were at
the college, she began to realise all the dying stages she had learn of
had happened:

'When we arrived, all the students were gathered. It was getting
dark. My dad and sister had flown in from Virginia. We all sat there,
on seats around the pool. They led the rosary and each one lit a
candle from the next one. All around the swimming pool were lit
candles. A circle of light.

'Many of the students came up. Each one had little things to say
about the last time they talked to Kevin, the last interaction. By the
time I had talked to more than one hundred, I had a sense of so many
particularly meaningful encounters between him and his college
mates. Younger ones in particular were supported.'

One girl in the college had been particularly isolated:

'She had a cocaine habit and she was hoping that by going to
college she would be away from it. She was struggling. Nobody
but Kevin recognised this. Privately, he helped her, he kept her
confidence. Later she wrote to me: *He got me through it. I am going to
be graduating with a college degree. Kevin did it for me.*

'One person he had spoken to told me he said, "You don't need
my help any more." It was as if he was a terminally ill patient going
through the last stages of illness but he was in the peak of health and
fitness. He was happy, it was his final year of philosophy, he was back
seeing his girlfriend. The last time they had been together was in
the chapel. She was happy with that; it couldn't have been in a better
place.'

Then Kathy put together the pieces of his final day. His adventure
day.

'The road had washed out. They're not used to that kind of rain in
Georgia. He got up and said: "We're goin' on an adventure."'

He and his male friends put on funny clothes and headed out. He
was like a pied piper. He had his T-shirt and jeans, a head warmer
with twigs in it. He was the only one not in shorts, a real Irishman.

They left their mobiles behind them, with a crowd of the girls. Kevin led all the way:

'It was as if he was being driven towards something. They were gone for a long time, crossing rivers, up hills, down valleys. They all said they had never seen Kevin so happy. He was a funny, funny guy, low-key in his humour. Nice and happy and excited, infectious.

'By the time they got to the lake, they were already tired. It was small so they often swam it. One of Kevin's friends, John Henry, swam it every day as part of his exercise routine. All of them hung back, except Kevin, because of the tiredness:

'But he said, "We've got to go across." Then he turned to John and said, "You know you're coming with me, because you always come with me." John jumped in and John Henry. Kevin was in his jeans, the only one who was, because he didn't like wearing shorts. The three of them headed across. The others stayed out.

'Then they just got into trouble out there, it was so cold. They struggled for a while and then realised they needed to head for shore. John and John Henry made it but they realised that Kevin wasn't making any progress so they went back for him. John Henry went unconscious three times trying to hold on to him. The last time he went under water he was holding Kevin's hand, just hanging on to him. When he came to, Kevin was gone. He tried to dive to find him, but he just wasn't there.

'Even to the end Kevin could feel that strength. He didn't die alone. He had someone holding on to him who loved him. A friend to the end.'

The difficulties arose from a combination of factors. Kevin was in jeans, which were harder to swim in. The lake was warm at the top and icy cold at the bottom but the weather had stirred up the colder waters and created problems with visibility. It had a shallow edge, but a very deep basin.

Kevin drowned a few feet from where he could have stood up. Even professional divers got into serious trouble that day and the next, trying to get down to retrieve his body, because of the water being so cold and churned up in the floods.

As Kathy speaks, I see Catherine at the water's edge, and know just what her psychic gift did for the families who had lost children to the water.

Kathy soon saw that she had been led to be as prepared as anyone can be:

'Putting it together, I realised how I had been prepared. I remembered from the final part of my death and dying research that the most important thing at the point of death is to create space for love. The people who love you here, the people who love you who have passed and God; that's what it's all about. You know, Kevin and I believed that. We are made for our relationship with God. It's a glove to a hand. A glove doesn't function until it's on the hand, then it's a perfect fit. Kevin had made his choice; he had chosen God.

'I was very conscious of the fact of John and John Henry carrying this load. They were deep friends, very close. They needed me to tell them they weren't guilty and couldn't have done anything. I sat down with them and told him that it was sudden, unexpected for all of us, especially for Kevin. But he wasn't unprepared. That last journey he went on, it was as if he was responding to a call. Confession, saying goodbye, going on a journey. With all this I just have to feel Kevin was ready; it was his time, I really appreciated that John Henry stayed with Kevin to the end, willing to sacrifice his own life to save his friend. My son.

'It's already taken me all these years and it'll take me more to be as ready as Kevin was.'

Those left at home had a difficult task, waiting for news, making arrangements. Rosalina, who helps with Kathy's son, Jamie, has lived with the family for many years. She dreamed that Kevin was dressed in white and wheeling his suitcase down the laneway, with Emma following him, trying to pull his suitcase back to the house. He was insisting, kindly, "I'm okay. I've got to go now. But don't worry, I'm really happy."'

The family are all grieving in their own way:

'Everyone is having their own journey. We talk a lot about Kevin; we have pictures around the house. But everybody is taking their own route. I think they're very conscious of the life they have now.'

Kathy's eldest son, Joady, had another inexplicable experience as he made funeral arrangements. His Italian wife Carolina received a text from him on her phone saying, 'Ciao, Piccolino. I've made it home. It's all good.'

'They had used that phrase all summer, my kids,' Kathy recalls.

Carolina answered, 'Glad to hear it.'

Joady found her text cryptic, so called her to see what was going on:

'He never sent that text. Carolina couldn't find anything but her reply when she searched her phone. She had pressed reply to Joady's message. But it was not in her inbox.'

Kevin continues to send messages to his mother:

'I wake up to him every morning. Before I open my eyes I think about him. I have such a sense of closeness to him as long as I pray. It's a real sense of coming close to the heart of Jesus and Mary.'

This is the blue love, shown in the eyes of those coming to this world and going from this world. I think of it as Kathy is driving away from my house, close to midnight, fuelled on a once-a-year coffee that will keep her awake all night, having once more given all she can. This is her nature.

I think of how direct her subscription to angels is, compared to my way of approaching and receiving messages. But I know why the heart of Mary is close to her. A mother who knows what it is like to lose a son and to have faith not only that she will see him again but that she sees him still. My faith doesn't need to be like Kathy's. But my heart has to grow to the size of hers before my own life journey is done, before I ask a palliative care nurse to pack a suitcase for me, so I can meet my angels.

I think now of the three women of this chapter and their prayer hands, holding on to the spiritual experience in the events that brought grief and the memories that bring joy. Good memories are angels. They help us to tell the stories of our time and to be part of the story, observer and participant, in birth, in death, in the life between.

9

Talking to the Dead

Dawn. A water's edge. A tall woman stands with the person in charge of those authorised to search. There are no houses nearby. The woman indicates this is the place she has seen in her vision. The co-ordinator radios the crew to come and dredge this section of water. The woman senses something and turns to find someone behind her. The coordinator reassures her to carry on. By the time her work and his work is done, a hundred more people have come to an isolated stretch, are standing on steep overgrown banks, watching.

Directly behind the tall woman is a family she has helped before. Someone they loved was found in the water. She has never met them face to face. The head of the search advises her who they are. She has a brief word with the mother and sister and moves on, back to her own mother and children, waiting in a car on the roadside.

One hundred people disperse.

Not one word makes it into newspapers as to how the body came to be found. Everyone by the water came to witness, not to spectate. The first family came to support the second family. The woman's gift has given both families bodies to bury.

I met her two years ago. She gave me a message then that shaped my life and gave me hope. Her days and her decisions revolve around her family, her business and long runs that help her to recognise the freedom in herself. The freedom she was born with. Sometimes we can be given spiritual abilities beyond our capabilities. Life can be about learning to adjust and manage them. Catherine was born with the gift and has spent a lot of her life dealing with it:

'I was seeing spirits at a very young age. I was a little kid of about seven in my grandparents' house. That's was the first time it really struck me because I could see these people, psychically see them, walking up the driveway and it frightened the living daylights out of me. I knew they weren't real.'

The visions fell away for a time. But they returned during her teenage years. Catherine has eyes the colour of sea. Piercing. Blue. She has an economy of phrase, so the full extent of what the returning meant can be seen only in how her eyes change, how they sharpen with the memories:

'And then the teenage years were a bit rough as well.'

Her mother, who found out, through Catherine's visions, about a secret, deceased aunt, incarcerated in an asylum for refusing to live with the man she was forced to marry, has been a source of huge support to her. The story of her mother's Aunt Rose made a bestselling book, *Restless Spirit*, written by Margaret Hawkins. Since then Catherine has gone on not only to acknowledge her gift but to develop it. Before Rose, she never specifically told her mother about the spirits she saw:

'I knew the difference between reality and what I was seeing. I tended to keep the seeing bit to myself, even as a kid. You don't want to be a freak, you just say you're scared and leave it at that. I used to have weird nightmares and my mother would say, "What was in the dream that scared you?" I couldn't tell her because it was just a feeling.'

As Catherine describes spirit visits she offers me a sponge cake, made the day before. Her daughter, who has the eyes of a fawn, is standing close to her. Her husband comes in to get some tea and go back out to dig over their vegetable patch.

The sense of other was there for her the whole time. She engages in practical tasks while explaining this:

'There's something else out there. Always I felt there was someone behind me or something behind me. You could say that's normal, everybody gets that, but I had it chronically for twenty-seven years. Couldn't sleep with the light off just because of this feeling.'

Even if Catherine wasn't talking about what she was seeing, her mother Patricia was sensing it and went as far as having her daughter's bedroom blessed.

'When I was a teenager I went through a really strong phase. Obviously this ability, whatever it was, was struggling to get out – I think adolescence does that. You know, the heightened emotions, this heightens with them.'

When she says 'this', she never points to anything, or mentions what 'this' is. I know properly, at this moment, how hard Catherine works to accept both this gift and the life that comes with it. A life of choosing friends carefully and avoiding those who would denigrate her for it or be desperate for her to use it with them. I am here as part of the angel journey but as she talks I realise that the message she gave me two years previously was all that I should need or ask for. I don't need a spiritual update. What she said two years ago stayed with me enough to see me through a terrible depression. In the middle of it I wrote a piece called 'Postcard from Mir' for an anthology. Not a piece about depression. A piece in depression. It had just been published. And Catherine told me something that came from someone I loved who died of the same disease I was suffering from. She gave me details about this man that convinced me she was communicating with him:

'You are just about to branch out. The hard work is done.'

That sentence got me through.

There are those who seek constant confirmation of their dead loved ones and in a way this is wrong: to expect a woman with a young family to talk to the loved we have lost. She describes mediumship as spiritual welding: welding the link broken by death. If spirits come to her with messages she will deliver them if the living person is open to hearing them. She has helped the authorities to find the location of two bodies. Bodies that would have been lost to their families without her help.

Catherine helped the first family at a time when no one but her mother knew what she saw:

'It was the turning point in terms of being public about what I do. I wouldn't admit to anyone, not to my own father, what I did. There was a guy missing and I kept looking at this missing poster in shops. I'd look at his eyes and say, "I know where you are." It used to hit me in my soul, deeper than my heart. I said it to my mum, and I described where he was. It was as if I could feel what he was feeling. It was real emotion.'

Catherine might have doubted her ability but her mother didn't. When the man still had not been found after three months of searching, she shared the knowledge with one friend, who contacted the search team. He spoke to their head, who agreed to take any information she had through a third party. This was Catherine's wish, to protect her anonymity, but more importantly she did not want the family of the missing man to have expectations of her information leading to the discovery of his body.

'The details I gave them made sense. So the crew head spoke to my mum. I never spoke to him directly. I just used to say it to my mum and she'd say it to him; it was like a three-way thing.'

After the first information she gave was considered useful, she became more confident in what she imparted:

'I described this man and what he was wearing and a piece of jewellery he was wearing. They went to check. So they sent a Garda to his mum's house. And they described what I'd said and she went, 'Oh, you've found him.' Because of what I'd said. Nobody knew about this piece of jewellery. She'd never mentioned it. And when they said it to her, she thought he was found. And that hit me. I was so shocked. I didn't feel good. I felt awful for doing that to her. For giving her that bit of hope that he was found. But even if he was gone I knew that she'd know what had happened to him.'

This reinforced her determination to help police and search teams to track down his remains.

'I told them what I had seen. On the basis of that they decided to search where I said: seven or eight men searching for five days and they didn't find him. It was a Wednesday evening, and I was here in this house, right in there' – she points to the living room. 'I remember being on my own, and crying, out loud, "You feckers, why did you give me this if it's no use? Why did you tell me all that stuff that fits, if it's absolutely no use in the end?" I was furious, with them, the spirits, whoever had given me this, for making all these poor people search, for breaking his mother's heart all over again. I felt so bad.

'I sent a text message to the coordinator, who'd trusted me the whole way and put this team on the search and I just apologised, because I thought I couldn't speak to him on the phone. I went to bed early, sobbing my heart out.'

She woke up the next morning and first thing the phone rang. The coordinator spoke to her directly for the first time. Two words:

'He's found.'

Even now, some years later, Catherine insists I don't describe what she saw. The details are with me and very precise:

'My dad's a very religious man. I thought he would never accept it but he gave me a hug and said, "You were doing good work." It was all he ever said about it. It was never mentioned again. And he still won't sit in the room if we're talking about stuff like this. But that was enough.'

By 'enough', Catherine means she allowed her ability to enter her life, instead of pushing it away from her. So when she had a call from the search coordinator about another case, she became involved.

'I was called back up by the same man to help to look for someone else. If there are angels walking on earth he's one of them, because of the work he does. He said, "Would you come up and help me look?" Whenever anyone goes missing, he lives it, heart and soul. He feels it. He understands it. He asked me to go up and I went up, quietly. Nobody knew about this. We went down to the bank of the river, because I had a particular area in mind.

'He wanted to bring me down to the last point where this person was seen and see if it was the same as what I was seeing in my head. I parked away from the water, so nobody would know. We climbed down the bank, just the two of us. He radioed the crew, to come up with the chains and do that area. Very quietly; nothing was said. The two of us were standing at the bank and I noticed there was somebody behind me. He told me it was all right.

'After about ten minutes I turned around and, spread up through the woods, at least a hundred people had quietly come to see what was happening. It frightened me because they all knew who I was; they knew why I was there. But the family of the first man was right behind me, standing behind me. That's when I realised the first man's family knew how he'd been found.' He was found in an area she had a vision of but, more than that, she described how he died. She has learned to hand over the information, regardless of how she feels about it:

'The coordinator said it to the family and they took great comfort from that. Now it could have gone the opposite way; they could have hated hearing it. But they heard, from what I said, that he didn't commit suicide.'

She continues to work for free. There is no reason why a mother of small children who runs a successful business, who never asked to see spirits, should put her valuable time into a notion she is making up. She only practises in:

'A very informal way, if I happened to be with somebody who's open. I can say, well, "I've got somebody here. He belongs to you. Do you want to talk about them?" My conscience couldn't handle taking payment.

The one thing with all psychic work and spiritual work is that it feeds your ego. Part of that is necessary because, if you're going to stand up in front of a room full of people and do a demonstration and be confident, you need a certain amount of ego.

'But when it oversteps a certain mark and goes beyond that, it's a problem and it's something you always have to keep in check. When you bring money into the equation, it's the ego that wants the money and it just doesn't fit with me: it feeds me in a very bad way and I can't do it. You just have to do it in the moment and then let it go. It's gone, it's done.'

The first time I met Catherine she said, 'Others have to have faith in an afterlife. I know there's an afterlife.' It was a very simple statement with an extraordinary reach. But the information that comes to her is the price she pays for the knowledge. She has learned to deal with this only after years of avoidance.

For a time, in the years of avoidance, Catherine was lost to herself: 'As a teenager I practically had mental problems, based on all this stuff as well. It does, it drives you mad.'

'My old house used to haunt me. I used to see things, hear things. I never felt safe there. It's a very old house anyway, in an old terrace,

right down in the centre of town. There was an old woman in the
doorway. My mum would say, "It's only a dream. It can't be she's still
there." The minute I'd go in my room and shut the door, it was an
oasis of calm after it was blessed. Everything used to stop at the door.
And then I went to college, which was a break I needed. It wasn't for
me but it gave me that space to go back and be a different person and
just get a job and settle into a normal life. And that's what continued.
Up to my late twenties.'

She learned to shut the door on it all the time but the difficulty
with this strategy was the running. Now Catherine runs all the time,
out of freedom. Then it was fear:

'The more you keep running away from this thing, the more
it scares you, the more of a big problem it is. The minute you turn
around and face it, it's like anything, it diminishes and becomes
something you can handle. Turn and actually have a look at it and
think, "What is this?" That's what happened with me.'

When did that happen? She stops warming up oil for chips and
turns on the cold tap to rinse her hands. I think she hasn't heard the
question. But then she says it happened when she was introduced to
Rose:

'Rose introduced herself to me. That was the point where instead
of running away from these presences I actually turned and I said:
"It's a person. They might be dead but they still look like a person." It
all changed from there. That put me on my right path.'

Twenty-seven years of pretending not to see came to a stop then.

It was on a Spanish holiday that Catherine and her mother,
Patricia, began to understand and truly communicate about her
psychic abilities. Rose came into the room as Patricia was speaking
about her and talked to the only member of her family who wanted
to find out she existed.

'From the beginning she just wanted her story told. She wanted to
be known.'

Does she ever see Rose now?

'She can make herself aware, you know, make herself known to
me, but she tends to stay out of my way, really; she doesn't need me.
When she comes through she's not the same person she was at the

start. She came through as a real person, with real problems at first, with real frustration and real anger, and she doesn't come through like that any more, she doesn't even look the same. Really, she doesn't have to show herself in that way. She just brings herself through as this wonderful, almost light that's always a kind of violet or lavender colour. That's how I know her. And if somebody else is giving me a link to her, they'll always bring that in, that colour: "She's wearing this beautiful purple colour." I know who that is. Even though she would never have worn it in life. She does that so I'll recognise her. Or she'll do the usual: "I can smell roses." That's how she gets her name across. She'll make them smell roses.'

It's an indication, perhaps, that the work Catherine did helped Rose to get to that stage? She sits down, after her multi-tasking, and takes a minute to answer this. This is another thing she does, weighing up her responses to make sure they are appropriate. I can feel the responsibility in it for her:

'It helped her. She was very connected to the family, trying to be brought back in. It was very important to her to close that gap and to heal the wound in the family as well. Once she had that done it's like she evolved, almost. She could let go of that persona and become her spiritual self.'

I'm thinking of those I spoke to who feel they've been overtaken or attacked by evil. What is Catherine's view of evil presence? Does she believe in or detect it?

'Now, I realise first off there's nothing out there to be scared of at all. Even if people talk about demons and bad spirits. I'm sorry: in my book, there are no bad spirits. There are very misunderstood spirits. Those maybe you wouldn't want to spend time with. You just say, "Let me be," and they have to. They can't plague you, they can't attach to you. You hear all this nonsense and it makes no sense to me because I've never experienced any of it. Even when I was frightened by these things, I realise now it was just somebody really wanting badly to communicate. They see you like a spark in the darkness and they hone in, thinking, "She'll hear me if I talk to her." That's all it is. How frustrated would you be if you were trying to talk to someone and they wouldn't listen? And kept running away from you?'

She doesn't smile often – or at all when she's on this subject, I'm smiling because I see a laundry basket full of folded running gear, from her latest hill run. I feel that the hills are where the burdens are left. I say listening can sometimes be a burden if you really hear what's said. It doesn't sound connected to anything she's saying. But she seems to get it:

'In terms of a spirit, yes. That's why I think people are frightened of them, because they come very close. And that's where all this stuff about entities, nasty stuff, originates. I've come across places that made me feel very unpleasant. Every time I come up against that I try to say, "No, hang on, that really isn't how it works for me."'

After Rose, Catherine became more aware of who was working with her and why. One man has been with her for ten years. Someone she calls, 'my man in black'.

'When I became aware of guides, I'm a terrible sceptic and I thought I'm not going to have guides.' But she realised one or two of the presences she was encountering were more than making contact: 'I just thought they were people. I had a woman called Elizabeth, who was actually the first. She was a protector, very like Rose. I think she's actually a great-grandmother of mine. I never saw her. I only ever saw her hand on my sleeve because she was always behind me. She watched my back and it was like she was bringing me through the initial stages and keeping me strong and pushing me a little. Any time I felt scared, I knew she was at my back. And then she faded away. And I became more aware of two gentlemen. One – I always laugh when I say it – looked like Einstein. He used to give me lessons and that's why he let me see him as Einstein. So I'd go, "Ooh, yeah, smart." Crazy but smart. And I'd relate to him.

'He used to bring me on these wonderful journeys and try to explain things to me and he always came in with the man in black. They were like a pair. Eventually, everybody else faded away and the man in black stayed. And he's been there the whole time.'

What about the journeys that Einstein took her on?

'They're very deep and you can't put them into words. They really are. If I try to explain them I'm going to sound like a lunatic.'

Catherine feels the guides were showing her concepts of how to understand time, how to understand our connection to one another, how to understand that we're all made of the same thing and go back to the same thing. That was all explained. They don't happen to her so often now. She feels that they came because she was starting off on her spiritual journey and very open and just let it happen:

'Whereas now I'm too aware. You have to be very free. The minute you're consciously aware, bang, it's gone. The minute you try and catch it, it's gone.'

But not entirely. She has realised this:

'Your spirit people are around you all the time and the more you do this work the more familiar you get with them.'

Since she began to develop her own mediumship skills through study abroad, Elizabeth and Einstein have moved away: 'I don't need them any more. They give you what you're missing until you get it yourself. You know, it's like strength, confidence. Einstein, that guy, he taught me these amazing lessons that I've never forgotten.'

She now practises what she describes as fearless mediumship, something she did when she passed on the circumstances of the second death in the water:

'You just say it, don't care who's looking at you, don't care if you're right or wrong, just say it and that's the phase I'm in at the moment. I force myself. If I'm seeing a pink teddy bear with one ear missing, well then, I'll say it, no matter how ridiculous it sounds. That's what he's saying.'

Not all her messages are about resolve; some are humorous: 'The funny ones lately – and I hope my mum won't mind me saying it – we were connecting to a relative of ours whom I know. I was trying to get her to reveal things I wouldn't know about her. So she brought my attention to her son, when he was a little boy, and she was showing me ping pong balls. I'm trying to interpret this. I said to my mother: 'Did he choke?'

'She said, "No, no." I said, "Right, I'll give it exactly as she's giving it to me. She's showing me the child, aged about two. He's not well and she's showing me ping pong balls. My mother started to laugh. He had a tumour on his testicle, hence the ping pong balls.

'My mother was the one who discovered it, which was why it was a connection for her. She was minding the child while his mother was in having her second son. This goes to show: don't interpret it, just say it, and the person will know exactly what it means. And don't think it's being ridiculous, just give. In a million years, my rational mind wouldn't dare to say anything like that.'

She doesn't know why she was chosen but she has an appreciation now of how spirits accept her entirely as she is, even if she struggles with this gift herself: 'They have to work with your own temperament and if I'm a kind of a polite person who doesn't talk about sensitive areas, well, they won't get me to give it.'

How do her guides connect to angelic energy? She laughs:

'A couple of years ago, I was struggling with this thing that everybody was into angels. I don't see angels. I don't see them as angels, at all. "What's that about?" I said it to my man in black. He has a great sense of humour. He was sitting with his elbows on his knees looking at me, and he said, "If you want angels, I'll be an angel." He turned so I could see his back, with this big pair of wings.'

'Spirits will manifest themselves in the form you feel comfortable seeing them. He told me, "For some people they're angels. For you that doesn't work so I'm something else, and if they want me to appear as an angel that's what I'll be. It doesn't mean I'm any of those things." I think they're beyond anything we can understand. They're not light. They're not angels. They're not spirit things. It's just something that we can't grasp.'

At the moment, the man in black keeps Catherine confident:

'We don't communicate enough because I keep my mind too busy at the minute. He'd really love me to be creative but I find it hard. I know the busier my head gets, the more I need it to be quiet. That's what's wrong. But he's always there. I always have an awareness of him. Anytime I'm feeling distracted or upset, all I have to do is go, "Stand beside me." And he does. He's very calming.'

It's interesting that she uses this adjective, because the last way I would ever have thought of describing a medium and her messages is calming. It's what Catherine is. I've met her three times and every time I leave her calmed.

The power of suggestion is a power. Anything can be implied and anything can be interpreted. How does she answer this? By agreeing.

'I think if I didn't have the spiritual thing I have I'd be the worst sceptic in the world. I'd be the one going out trying to burn witches. They call it machine-gun mediumship, "I've got a woman for you, she says something about a purple ring, and I've got a man for you and he's wearing a flat cap," and, "Oh yeah, there's a gentleman over here for you and he used to drive a blue car." What use is that to anyone?

'I have to question it, even in myself. It really has to prove itself to me beyond everything before I actually accept it.'

Where does she think she is going with this?

'At the moment I don't care. I used to care. I used to think, I'm meant to do something with this. I'm meant to be this, that or the other. But I don't care. To be honest, what I've found out is that what I do with this is completely irrelevant. It's what it makes of me. Because everybody is on their own journey through life. We all came here for a reason and we've to learn our own lessons. And it's the person it makes me into that's more important.

'If that means I drop it' – we never call it anything other than 'this' or 'it' – 'but still turn into a very spiritual person and am the person I'm meant to be, that's fine. I simply don't care any more.'

It's a huge responsibility. She nods her head:

'Massive. The main thing is to leave people uplifted and supported. That's the phrase that you have to keep in your head. Remind yourself all the time, "Have I left this person more damaged than they were at the beginning or have I left them uplifted and supported?"

Catherine had an aunt who died recently who made contact with her: 'Her words were: "It's not such a bad journey after all." That's how she put it across to me. I can't even explain it. It's an emotion you're given as well. "It's not such a bad journey after all." She was saying it in a very relaxed state. She died of an illness – obviously it wouldn't have been nice – but she said that was all just bringing her here. So none of it was bad, you know, the whole passage.'

Wherever 'here' is, wherever angels dwell, is worth the pain of living to reach. What a calming sensation to have within you when you leave a house. A woman with no time has given me her day to help me on my journey. I leave with less doubt.

By the time I leave her family is around the table waiting for the dinner she is late making. I don't know how she moves between the two worlds.

Driving, thinking. Remembering Catherine's words and also Bernadette's. Call them angels. Call them what you like. It's all the same thing. It's what we hear when we pray.

An angel journey is not so much about angels as about where looking for them takes you. I've been all over Ireland. I've slept in the back of my van. I've watched stars and made decisions. I've tried to screw this up the whole way. But it all comes back to three words.

I believe her.

Some people sleep more comfortably tonight because of Catherine's calm and her messages.

I am one of them.

10

COMING ALIVE

Don't ask what the world needs. Ask what makes you come most alive, because what the world needs is people who have come alive.

Howard Thurman

Catherine shows me the garden. Her husband Neil made it with his bare hands out of the grieving for their daughter Jessica. He dug the earth by hand and lifted boulders of granite and quartz into position on the mounds. He put in a pond and fountain and placed a standing stone at the end of a willow walkway. For Jessica. He built a patio, with a granite bench and the words: 'To Our Itty Bitty Girl'. It's the kind of inscription you see on benches in parks, when the grieving want their place on earth remembered. Jessica's room is a conservatory leading on to the patio.

'No one who met her was left unaffected. She had a way of changing people.'

The experience of Jessica's life and death, ten miracle months, brought the family alive. They believe in angels. They had one and they lost one. They also know their house is full of Jessica and those spirits who came to assist.

Catherine gave Jessica life and then gave her life again in the months she helped her to stay alive. In turn, the message that Jessica delivered to Catherine was to gain for herself all the belief she had for her daughter.

Lissencephaly, which literally means smooth brain, is a rare brain-formation disorder, resulting in a lack of development of brain folds and grooves. There are varying degrees of the condition. It affects other vital organs. In Jessica there was no reason, according to the specialists, why she should have survived in the days after birth, such was the deterioration of her kidneys. Respiratory problems are the most common cause of death. Catherine and Neil and their son Christopher lost Jessica physically but never spiritually and in her going they found a new sense of one another:

'I can't even express what holds people together at times like this. There's something beyond love. Deeper than love. It gets you through. Love is a word people use too much and people don't even know why they're saying "love". To get through what we got through goes beyond love, to a connection I have no words for.

'We thought they were talking about someone else's child at first. Not our beautiful girl. We were rushed to Temple Street Hospital and they thought she wouldn't even make it there alive.

'The head neurologist had great empathy with us; she didn't believe Jessie was strong enough to leave Temple Street. She thought she was just going to die up there at three weeks old. Jessica proved them wrong; oh by God, she proved them wrong. They said she wouldn't have any control over her limbs. But you can see from the photos in the hall she never stopped. We got to take her home.

'She had so much interaction. I didn't care where it was, we went with Jessie. O'Brien's cafe in Arklow, a woman called Tracey there, when she saw us coming she made sure we had a couch and space for Jessica's gear. She had no fear of asking someone to move. There were feeders to go up, oxygen cylinders, the works. If you didn't like the tubes, get over it.

'Old ladies came to say: "She's a fine girl, she'll be grand."'

'Doctors said to me that she would never be able to react, never be able to follow me around the room with her eyes or do anything with her body. She was watching her mobile when she lay on the floor and pulling her legs up. She was able to move her head. I have it on camera. I have her cooing on my phone, talking back to me. She smiled at us. I reckon if I had listened to the medical experts I'd have left her in her cot and done nothing with her and just made her comfortable. They said because she didn't have a gag reflex she would never be able to eat or drink normally and that she would always have to be fed by tube and hydrated intravenously. She was eating sweet potato and carrot and loving it. I remember one day she became a glutton and had wind pains. I felt so glad for her that she was having the experience of having eaten too much, instead of having never eaten at all.

'We had good months. She was well right up until March of the following year. Then she got her first dose of pneumonia. She came out of that dose but in May she started to deteriorate again. The doctor said the time had come for me to make a decision, to put her on life support and prolong her life but never have her at home with us again or to let nature take its course.

'I said she'd had enough, of prodding and poking and hospital and pulling. We took her home.'

For her last nine days. Jessica had a suction machine to keep her airwaves clear and two cylinders of oxygen. The oxygen delivery man thought he was delivering to an old age pensioner who had smoked all their life. When he saw Jessie he rang the hospital, convinced they'd made a mistake. He had never seen a child needing that much.

'On the last day of her life, when I was holding her constantly, a friend took her while I went to the toilet and she went bananas at me when I left her and even more so when I came back. She was letting me know she didn't want to be without me.

'My birthday was on 16 June. She gave me until six o'clock. And then she changed and things changed. She was so bad two friends had to leave, they couldn't cope. I completely understood. At ten o'clock she got more upset. At four the next day, the palliative care nurse came and asked if I realised that she was dying? I didn't. I couldn't see how ill she looked. The nurse said she hoped she was wrong but we should prepare ourselves.

'I put my head on the pillow beside her. Christopher came up at six in the morning, and got his dad to come down to his bedroom. Her temperature rose. I gave her medicine and can still see the stain on her pyjamas. I lay beside her and she died. I had prayed that we would all be asleep and she would go peacefully.'

By the time Catherine has shared the story of Jessica's life and death we are both in tears. The truth of the saying, if you follow the spirit of your life you never know where it will lead you, is borne out in the life of this powerful little being and those who were in family with her. As she began to move on from physicality, the rise in thoughts and impressions around her, which Isabel, in 'The Blue Love', speaks about in the time leading up to her daughter Paula's death, indicated there was more to the dying than the ending of life. A sensation of beginning occupied the room.

'That was it. She left us. As she was dying I saw her looking at spirits in the room. Staring at them. This house was packed with spirits. You felt you were in the way. Neil was feeling and seeing them too. There was a woman in the hallway; we saw her several times. It was beyond ridiculous. Neil saw them even more than me. People always question the spirits being around at the point of death. But they were there. The spirits are ordinary people but people who are not here any more.'

Neil had a clear vision of two spirits leading their son Christopher from his bedroom at six am to get Neil to come down to him, so that he had someone with him when Jessica passed, and also that Jessica had Catherine to lie with her as she left this world. It was a painful moment but one full of beauty, love and presence. The story of Jessica's life is also the story of a rise in awareness in her mother. She feels that the pain she experienced opened new doors to this awareness. I never want to know what it is like to a carry a white coffin, as Jessica's father did, and place it in the ground. I never want my sons to go through what Christopher went through when his sister died. He came into the room where she was and left quickly, saying to his grandparents, 'Don't go in. There's a sad story happening in there.' Then, when he saw Jessica laid out in her coffin, he began to sense what Catherine and Neil already knew: 'She's in her treasure box.'

Jessica brought her mother and father on a journey to the deepest:

'I had spiritual insight before but I didn't know what it was. I was meant to go through that to get here. Before Jessica I didn't think much of myself in every aspect and I let myself down in a lot of ways. I had no respect for myself, I suppose. All my life I had been saying, "I can't," so I wouldn't let anyone say it about her. I knew the capabilities of her body in medical terms. I knew about her anatomy and physiology. But there is more to people than their physical being.

'I took a leaf out of Jessica's book. She came with a purpose and she fulfilled it. I can't express how much strength I got from being her mother. Not just me. She changed a lot of people. Without Jessica I would never have done what I did.'

That was just the beginning. In the past two years Catherine has trained as a special needs assistant, in healing using the energy from angels, Reiki healing using human energy, various massage techniques and hopi ear candling.

'I can see big changes in me and Neil. I saw things in black and white. I let rip if people annoyed me. Even in our relationship, we had forgotten how to treat the other person. I realised there is more to life and more to people. I steered my life in a different way. I never spoke about what I saw or felt. Now I am open about my spirituality. I talk openly about God and spirituality. It has made me a more confident person. If there is something I firmly believe in I won't let it drop. I have more compassion for people. I have thought more about myself and how to improve myself.'

The key moment in letting Jessica go was when Catherine came to a workshop organised by Bernadette, who features in 'Forgiven'.

'She's a woman to be trusted. She has been through so much and she gives more than she takes. I decided to train in angel energies with Bernadette and it was during my second attunement that I found myself deep in a visionary experience that has never left me. For a week afterwards I didn't move outside my hall door.

'I felt myself going through a meadow. I could feel the wind. Then over a bridge across water. Then on to the beach at Brittas Bay without a fear. Her ladyship with me. All these energies. Flying. Angelic. No faces or wings. The sea is a golden fire, sun setting. That kind of warmth is in the day. We're up on the sand dunes. I have her in my arms and can feel her hair. A fiery haze over the sea, a band on the horizon.

'Up to this point I could feel myself in Bernadette's room. Then I joined the surroundings and the journey was for real. I could feel my baby girl as if she was still here.

'I could see images of family members who had died. Then an energy that felt so extraordinary I felt it was God. The energy went to take Jessica and I wouldn't let her go. I said, "No," because I didn't know who or what the energy was. I refused. Then Alan came. He was a cousin of Neil's who had died of leukaemia. He reached out to her and I let him take her and they walked away from me. I was so ill, so distraught. I was ready for it, but the loss...I wasn't well at all. But I was content because I knew who took her. It was Alan. He was a prankster who died too young. Like Jessica. I could see them and I let it happen. But when I came out of it, it wasn't good, I had to let her go.

'There's a picture on Bernadette's wall of an adult leading a child away into the distance. The minute I opened my eyes I saw it.'

The picture is the one I sat in front of, in Bernadette's room, painted by an artist who gave me one of my life messages. I tell Catherine this and her eyes shine:

'The connections. That painting. It's done work on two of us.'

We came away from Bernadette's with new purpose and a sense of life being more. For me the sense was the connections of humanity, the angel pathways between us; for Catherine the connection to angelic beings and properties was only just opening up. She has come alive:

'Until that day Jessica obviously still needed me and I needed her too. Not a question. Now she has moved on. But she belongs with us. If we go on a family day out, we tell her to come with us. We were on our way to Dublin once and all of a sudden my phone, which was in my bag, started to play a video of her clapping.

'But you don't need lotions and potions or any tricks. You just need to close your eyes and go into the quiet space. That is God. That's the place where angels leave their messages.'

Changing lives. How does it come about? How do you go from being one person to another? Like Catherine, this is a characteristic of the individuals in 'Coming Alive'. They have all moved in the direction of training in therapies.

Before I go to see Mary, I spot a collection of Chinese folk tales, beautifully illustrated with brush-stroke paintings, waiting to go on to a shelf in my library. I picked these up in a second-hand shop the previous week and something tells me to take a couple to Mary. Her sister introduced us so I haven't realised at this point that she is trained in and practises Chinese medicine. I reject the idea, saying aloud, 'Why would she want those?' I take a candle with me instead.

I tell her this and she laughs, because she has just started to practise Chinese brush-stroke painting and calligraphy. Mary's first experience of realising there was spirit and the synchronicity of things was many years ago, in Australia:

'I was very scared really. I came in from work and lay down on the bed, then started travelling almost immediately, in a way I couldn't recognise as dreaming. I found myself in a place I recognised as China, although I'd never been there. An old man came straight up to me and met me in the eyes. I came back to my bed then. I got a right fright: it was so overwhelming that I never forgot it or spoke about. I got up to get my tea and told myself I was just overtired.

'At the time I had no connection with China, or idea of it. But twenty years later it came to pass that I went there. I had decided to train in Chinese medicine and the first things I saw when I arrived were the places I had seen in the travelling experience. I remember saying to myself, "If this old man appears now I'm ready to be gobsmacked."

'He was the director of the college I was studying in and the first time I saw him he appeared exactly as I had seen him. The day I graduated I got a special award and he presented it to me. He got the translator to tell me he had made a special piece of calligraphy for me: '*Always uphold good. Always bring honour to the gift you have*'.

'The translator struggled to give me any more of a translation than that but he stopped her and said, "This woman already knows. We've met before. We're old souls." He had seen me too. There was no boundary of time. Twenty years later we were meeting in the flesh. He remembered me and I remembered him. I feel certain there was a connection there, a communal feeling, of angels bringing us together. Forces help us to join others in humanity with the same calling.'

Mary had decided to train in Chinese medicine, not just because she had this travelling episode. In fact she ignored it in favour of other things that were more tangible and built a successful clothing business:

'I was just working as a businesswoman and I had been getting a feeling for a while of knowingness and arriving in strange places, knowing I had been there before. My husband was a medical practitioner. As people came into his surgery, I would know what would be wrong with them. There weren't too many people I could speak openly to about this knowledge, my husband included.

'Now people have less of an issue with this kind of knowing but then it was considered mental illness. It got so bad, I went to the priest to ask for guidance and he told me to check into John of God's. I began to question myself as to whether this was happening. I left the presbytery crying and again became very frightened and I remember saying, "I don't know if I believe in you any more. You need to help me with these insights. You have to teach me who you are and assist me in this. Send me help."

'About a week later there was a knock on the door and this ordinary-looking woman was outside it. "I think I have the right house," she said. "I was sent to give you help." Her name was Josie and she was a healer from a neighbouring county. I had never set eyes on her, nor she on me, but she had been driving by the house and said to her companion that she had seen it in a dream and knew she was to call in.'

Mary's journey began and she has never looked back. From the moment she decided to train, her life's work unfolded as if she had always been meant to do it. She still had work to do on withstanding the criticisms that come with an open expression of using energies in your life and existence. But she has done her work and stands firmly in her faith consciousness. As with the women mystics in 'The Unnamed', her chief leaning is: 'love, despite and because of everything'.

Iris, who is a financial controller, has always kept good accounts on what people think of her beliefs and expressions of faith. From a young age she simply didn't care. When I visit her in her Kildare home she offers me an angel statue with the word 'love' inscribed on it. Immediately I think of Mary.

'When I was about thirty-six I knew it was my time, after having my family, to explore and allow myself to expand and grow. I always felt there was an inner longing for something else. One thing after another started falling into place. Rather than being a physical being having a spiritual experience, you're actually a spiritual being having a physical experience and everything that goes with that.

'I did a six-day course in angelic energies, then decided to do my teacher-training course. It was one of the most life-changing experiences of my life. Everybody was on the same wavelength, on the same path.

'There have been so many messages for me. I'll tell you a lovely experience if I may. I can't remember how it came about. It would be unusual for me to alone for this period of time. My husband used to travel quite a bit with work, so there would be periods when he would be away. I was on my own all day Friday, all day Saturday. And on Sunday morning I was reading the book. I was really into reading this book. I hadn't had any contact with the outside world whatsoever. I got to the chapter about unconditional love.

'I asked would they please give me a shower of love. I have never experienced anything like it. It started at the very top of my head. Every cell, every pore in my skin moved. Every part of my being was revitalised. It started and the whole thing, it came right down over my whole being. I was sitting there with that wonder, that awe. And I could feel, like a progressive thing, all the way through, every cell, every particle of my being moved and shifted. And when it got to the base of my toes I thought, "Oh my God, that was the most amazing thing ever." It was as if I had been touched by an angel. It absolutely left me without a shadow of a doubt that I had had a spiritual experience.'

Iris tells me about other experiences. They sound like her, good to the core. She has made the decision not to earn money, because for her the joy is in giving, as it is for Catherine in 'Talking to the Dead':

'I love connecting to spirit. I love reaching out and teaching about spirit. If I can help somebody to open up to spirit, the sense of reward and everything that goes with that is phenomenal, it's wonderful. But I don't want it to be my job. If I have to earn in order to do it, it takes something from it for me. I get so energised and energetic and so filled up when I connect to spirit, when I'm talking about angels. I feel the energy change in the room when they are present. It's amazing. I don't think anybody should charge for that.

'There are so many extraordinary experiences I could talk about for hours. Five years ago, I was diagnosed with a pancreatic tumour. With my absolute belief in the power of the angels and the ability to self-heal, the tumour is gone and I am here five years later. I look back now and I wonder sometimes if I imagined half of it because it seems so huge.'

Iris, a rock of sense, also had one of the country's top oncologists assisting her. She laughs when I say that angels can be oncologists too. God gave us the medical profession:

'My liver function tests were all through the roof. I couldn't eat a morsel of food for weeks and weeks. I couldn't eat at all. I was very ill. I was collapsing, falling down. When I went back after six months the oncologist said to me, "Oh, we must have misdiagnosed that. There is no way you had a tumour if you're still here."

'But I knew the journey that had taken place.'

Then she tells me to listen for the sound of my children's laughter. It's the first thing I hear after a long drive home.

Eibhlin also chooses not to earn revenue from her practice as a complementary therapist. She considers that the way she lives now released her from a cage she couldn't otherwise find a key for. She also has a successful career in broadcasting.

'I slowly shifted thirteen years ago. I would have been involved in left-wing politics, an agitator. I would have been a right bolshie bitch. I would have been at war with the world in lots of ways. And yet, like most people who are bolshie, underneath there was softness and vulnerability. But I couldn't show it. Self-protection. Defensiveness.

'With perspective now, looking back, when I see my evolution as a persona, because we create our persona and we change it every few years, underneath it are the same core, vulnerability and issues – whatever your issues are. But I think we learn different coping strategies.

'When you see fourteen-year-old kids on buses they're all very brash and brittle. And they always speak exactly the same. They dismiss anything soft, anything vulnerable. That's the starting point, when you start creating your persona. It's all about self-protection. I did a huge amount of projecting my angst outwards into the world. I hated this or I fought that or this attracted me. It was a lack of introspection in lots of ways, in an empowering way. You live through fighting other people's battles for them. Then suddenly things started stirring in me. What really started the process was a dream and it wasn't like a dream, it was like a waking reality.

'I had been through all the various incarnations of punk, republican, socialist. Leather jackets and punky hair. That's how I was known where I work, as well. I was fierce. Then I had this dream in which I was in this white space. It was so real. It was as if I had woken up into reality and it wasn't like a dream at all. There was a huge golden hand coming down toward me and getting nearer and nearer and as it got nearer I knew that it was to do with healing. I went into bliss. It was incredibly intense. Remember that Lotto thing, "It could be you." That's exactly what the image was. A big golden hand coming down on to my forehead.

'I had awareness in the dream, in the reality. I stood back and was looking at what happened and had a sort of wonder moment. When I came to, I knew that I'd be healing. That was the start of everything.

'It was a momentum then that just took its own journey. I was full of wonder for ages. I was eating up books. I was reading and doing course after course in healing schemes and then more conscious therapies. It's been thirteen years of doing different therapies, to discover that the gradual process of unfoldment needs no words or certificates. It just needs to be allowed. 'People come for help and they are just like a younger me, very spiky and defensive and vulnerable. I can see right through that. Everything I've been through is stored there as a useful experience. I think that the clients you attract always relate in some way to what you've done for yourself.

'My own journey is primarily about reaching a place of connection and balance and joy within myself. Anything else is incidental. This doesn't mean that I'm being selfish but the universe starts with me. I am my own best client.'

Since Eibhlin and I both work in the media, we know spiritual pursuit is either the subject of fascination or contempt, sometimes both. Interestingly, she is grateful for her media savvy, as I am. We know how difficult it can be to define the indefinable. Equally we are aware of those who have appropriated and exploited airtime for what is allegedly their vision and actually their gain.

'My working life has helped me to filter what is authentic and what isn't. If you're grounded and ordinary you're going to have a much wider base of connection with people. You're coming from somewhere real that people can relate to. But if you have flown off into the light, there's a sense of denial of the ordinary there and there's also a sense of lack of being grounded. Some of the most spiritually aware and connected people are the most grounded people. And those who are meditating all the time and not eating, they're living in cloud-cuckoo land. They're not bringing their spirituality into this world where we all are. They may as well be gone. I'm here to live. I think, for an awful long part of my life, I didn't really want to be here. I was battling the world. I did not come to earth until I started working with energy and spirit.'

Does she bring her values to work with her? When she is out there earning a living?

'I do bring this to work. Other people, it took them a while to adjust. I'm open about my spiritual journey but I wouldn't be going around talking endlessly about it. There is no better way to live, even if self-doubt comes in every so often. But something will happen, some realisation will allay any doubts you have.'

As James said in 'Fallen Angel', about fear, doubt is the friend of the angel journey. It allows us to filter, as with Eibhlin, and find the authentic. It encourages us to call for help, so we meet our secret selves longing for air, as with Mary. It has allowed Iris to stay true to her loving nature and offer healing for the exchange of mutual good rather than gain and it gave Catherine the challenge that angel Jessica helped her to meet, the challenge of finding you are worth fighting for.

11

Time Stopped

A common thread to all the people I spoke with was an understandable measure of doubt: no matter how powerful their experience, they question it. This is the human condition. Fear and doubt are companions on the uncertain journey.

Still there are moments where entirety takes over. Some of the moments in this chapter are that. All are life-framing. Time slows, stands and takes a picture of circumstances that remains intractable. Whether you are atheist, Catholic, Buddhist or worship sofas, moments outside time exist for us all.

Then there are moments of great beauty and peace, like those in 'New Rooms'. Others involve protective forces that release the participant from danger. The inner guide says: be afraid. When I left the mountains around Machu Picchu, where I spent a day sitting in a cave under the ruined city, to go back to reality, I stayed in a luxurious hotel outside a humble town built and perpetuated only for the service staff who catered for the tourist. It was called *Aguas Calientes,* meaning Warm Water. It was New Year's Eve. My experience of it was cold. Checking in, I saw a man looking at me: well dressed, urbane, reading a literary novel. His eyes told a different story from his body. I was drawn to talk to him but repelled by something I didn't fully understand.

Later that night the power went out in the district. My travel companion and I decided to leave luxury to walk along the train tracks to a pizzeria in the town, to be with real people, in a real place. This man appeared from nowhere, walked up to us in the lobby and asked if he could join us? No one else was going into town, into darkness.

On each side of the track there were petrol-soaked rags alight in empty tins, at intermittent points. It was a beautiful sight and one of the worst nights of my life.

I have never met anyone evil before or since and I've encountered people who have spent most of their lives in prison, people who destroyed. This man was not sinister in his speech but he was disturbed in his energy. He was rich, powerful and avoided ruin through his intellect. His job was to go across the world telling people they were fired from jobs they had had for decades. He loved it. He loved the look of fear that crossed the person's face as they sat down in his office. It gave him a thrill. He had been a leftie in the sixties. Marched. Protested. He was done with altruism. The human race was done. He had left a wife who had a disability, left their daughter to care for her.

I was cold, more afraid than I can remember being. Time stopped. I knew I had to get away from him, break social convention, stand up and leave. I couldn't move. I was frozen. If angels fall, then I had a sense he was once a fallen one. I tried to protect my evening, my views and myself: "The next time you fire someone, look into their eyes, and try to see what's there."

By the time we walked back the rags had burned out; we had to feel our way from sleeper to sleeper on the train tracks. When we got back he suggested drinks. I argued with my travel companion that I wanted nothing more to do with him. I went to bed early and left them to ring in the New Year together. My companion came back to the room before midnight.

'He says people like you are proof that all the best people left Ireland, that only the dregs are left behind.' By now my travel companion had the same opinion of the man. But it was too late. He had done his work of dividing us.

I didn't answer. The following morning I went back up to Macchu Picchu, alone and met a Vietnam veteran on the bus. I found myself telling him the story. He said: 'You just met a violator. You meet assholes but that guy violates. You protected yourself from these people. Pain is their pleasure to inflict.'

Today I have no trouble saying that my spirit met his and fought.

He left me with memory. Memories are angels. If I ever get that sensation again I will run. That sense of silence, of time stopping and slowing down, of a picture being framed, accompanies some key spiritual moments.

Donna is not one to turn away from adventure. She has been all over the world and has had many spiritual experiences. She identifies her spirit guide thus:

'The first thought that comes into your head when you meet someone. Other people recognise it as instinct but I think it's your guide telling you what situations are good and bad for you. It just takes over your body and gets you out of there. Mine has saved my life three times.

When I left home at fifteen I got a place in a house, clearing in return for room and board. Things weren't good at home. The woman who took me in never gave me any grief; she kept me safe. A really good woman. No one can tell me that wasn't spiritual intervention. I was so young anything could have happened to me. But the spirit led me to a house of protection.

'She had DVDs to be returned, I took them back for her one night and was walking along a country road back out to the house which was just outside the town. A car came round the bend and went past me. My voice guide said, "Notice this." Other cars had passed me. But this one was different. The next thing I knew it was turning round and heading back in my direction.

'It went so silent, all around me.

'Out, like an SAS person, the spirit guide comes, and before I even have time to think I turned on my heel and ran up the road and dived into the hedge, burying myself in it. It was a hawthorn hedge. The car stopped, two guys got out and started to poke about in the hedge. They were shouting that they knew I was there and they were going to kill me when they got hold of me. I was sitting there, making an act of contrition, "I am so sorry for all I have done." I was expecting to die at that moment. They're going to pull me out of the hedge by my head and do away with me.

'They drove off. They came back again. I stayed in the hedge, not daring to move, for hours. I walked home through the fields and only turned up on to the road to run into the house. By that stage it was getting light and they were long gone.'

Jeanne was going through a painful divorce and her husband's family were behaving in a threatening way. He was a very successful lawyer who had emptied their business and personal bank accounts and stopped all her cards. The only thing he could not do was extract her from their family home. So he kept two people in cars posted outside it, to watch her movements. If she left the house he had a locksmith on twenty four-hour alert. The Gardai could do nothing. A man can do what he wants in and with his own home. He had said only that he was going to change the locks. You can't arrest someone on intent. Some friends and her own relatives helped her by dropping around food. The utility bills were left unpaid and the electricity was turned off.

'The only time I could get out was at night, when the cars went home. I couldn't rely on charity forever. I just sat and wept. I knew I couldn't stand up to this level of abuse. My mind was going.'

For the years she and her husband had lived and worked together, Jeanne had always shown kindness to the travellers who called to the door. In her business, she also served their needs free of charge. She not only respected them but learned from her conversations about spirit with them over the years.

As the weeks wore on Jeanne was left more and more alone. Her pride wouldn't let her reveal how awful her situation was. Her family, while supportive, had their own lives to lead and to protect them she hadn't let them know how abusive the relationship had become.

'I was left penniless. I couldn't call anyone. I was too vulnerable to think straight or fight back. So I got down on my knees and prayed for some help, from somewhere. I felt a sense of peace, a silence that came over my thoughts.

'When I got up I went to the kitchen to make some tea. There was nothing in the fridge and no way to heat the house. I couldn't believe my life had come to this. I had a sense I was going to have to leave with nothing but the clothes I stood up in. I was literally barricaded in.

'Then the kitchen door was knocked on. I was so afraid in case it was one of those my husband had paid to watch me come and go. But a voice said, "Open it." Outside was a traveller, who introduced himself and said he had been at mass and had a message come to him in prayer to come to my place. I told him I had nothing left to offer. He said he wasn't there for that.'

The man said to her: 'I got a message to help you, missus. This is all I have. I'll bring back more when I have it.' The man left Jeanne a small note of money on the table. He left more than that. She lost the panic, the sense she was going under. To this day she doesn't know if he just happened to call or was brought to her. But this act of kindness helped both her self-belief and her belief in others enormously. She has a new life on her own terms.

Caroline has a key memory of a visit to her grandmother's home in Belfast in the 1980s:

'I was going shopping to a large store in the city on a hot, sunny morning. It was a busy main street, within walking distance of shops and houses. A typical Saturday morning: people bustling round, food shopping; harassed moms laden down with bags and children; elderly folk with their single shopping bags. The general mood was jovial, with lots of noise.

'Then everything round me went deathly quiet. It was as if I was in a vacuum. It lasted only a split second. The silence was like walking into a strange, empty room. Although I was aware of cars and passersby, I couldn't hear noises associated with them. It wasn't deafness because the silence was a noise. It was a busy scene. As if you were watching TV with sound off. People all looked the same. I had no bodily sensations, just felt rooted to the spot and devoid of thought.

'Then I found myself turning back and going to local shops, not really knowing why. It felt I had no choice in the matter. I was gently being pulled away. Also you tend to grow a thick skin in that kind of environment, the Troubles, to have a life.' Caroline thinks still about why she didn't call out to others. She would have done if she had known what was coming next: 'But it was as if I had no thought, nothing really to contribute.

'On the way home I felt a slight tremor. I got into Granny's and she was very relieved to see me. The department store I was heading to and would have been in was blown up. I definitely believe it was my grandfather looking after me. We had a close relationship, regardless of the respect expected and the boundaries common between the generations at the time. The key incidence of it was that I took my first steps for him. I loved and trusted him before I could even speak. No matter where I went – I lived in various parts of the world – I never felt as much at home as I did when I was there, in his house.'

She has a great interest in Buddhism and a certain part of her grandfather's compassion and serenity reminds her of the Dalai Lama. In her story, in her framed moment, I am reminded of him saying: 'Compassion is not religious business, it is human business. It is not luxury, it is essential for our own peace and mental stability, it is essential for human survival.' The modesty and sympathy her grandfather was known for, Caroline believes, protect her spirit and interests today.

For Brona, time stood still when she was diagnosed with cancer. She has been an angel on my journey, assisting me with this book. Her own moment, her own snapshot, was significant. She describes it below, but also, having listened to others share theirs, she has valuable ideas about what spirit means and what messages mean: how time works and how the people in it relate to one another without words or physicality:

'I was brought up a Catholic. Catholic school. Catholic home. Prayers at bedtime. Mass on Sunday. The rule in my family was, 'You go to mass until you're eighteen, then you can decide.' At eighteen, I left the church behind and never looked back. I have created my own way to celebrate events and comings of age.

'So, in listening to interviews for *Angel Journey*, I expected to shake my head as people described angels flying in from the stars. Miracles from supernatural forces. Instead, I found I could relate to each story. All are exploring their sense of self, on their own. All are willing to break the rules and listen to their own voice, all certain of a wonder, a mystery, a sense of awe. Some define it as spirit, some as actual spirits. Some define it as God. I would have said I don't believe in God. I defined myself as an atheist. Yet what I hear in these interviews makes sense to me. I understand exactly as people describe their wonder. I know the sense of mystery. I am in touch with it more, having been ill recently. In love with life. Time and space to feel and explore and ponder me.

I feel all the things described: messages, coincidence, energy, love. I just define them differently. I am happy for them just to be me, just to be my subconscious, just to be my life force. Perhaps my soul, as long as it's not some entity separate from me that will fly away when I die. Once the concepts are outside me I find it hard to follow them. Something supernatural, out there, above, beyond; it stops making sense for me.

'In hospital I had inexplicable experiences of my energy as colour. I've had experiences of reflexology and Reiki in which I saw beautiful, bright, flowing purple and white light. My awareness and acceptance of death have allowed me to pay better attention to life. My sense of wonder is often overpowering. I have a new sense of history, of connectedness. My family's story is suddenly important. I have a need to understand where I've come from. I want to know more about my culture. I want to find out about women. I want to learn and experience. What I feel is me. What I know is me. Where are my experiences from or how to explain them? I accept that I don't have answers. It's impossible to know. And that's okay with me.'

Often the inexplicable nature of certain moments brings those subject to them to a place beyond words. As the thirteenth-century-Sufi poet Rumi said:

> *Out beyond ideas of wrongdoing and rightdoing,*
> *there is a field. I will meet you there.*
> *When the soul lies down in that grass,*
> *the world is too full to talk about.*
> *Ideas, language, even the phrase 'each other'*
> *doesn't make any sense.*

One of the chief obstacles to providing written accounts of spiritual messages is that they don't translate well to public scrutiny.

Small happenings, visualness can be carried in consciousness more easily than conversation.

Sarah, who shares a story of a close friend's death, is keenly aware of this:

'I find that I experience more than I understand or can articulate. There were many times throughout my earlier years when my knowledge of God was confirmed for me. For example, there was the time when an older close family friend was dying. Each and every member of my family received some kind of message and confirmation of God's existence with his passing. It was so profound that we still speak of it, over twenty years later.

'I was seventeen at the time and I remember when he was very close to death, I had visited this friend in hospital to say my goodbyes. As I was leaving, a stranger in the lift handed me a pot of flowers before getting off at their floor. I do not remember in what context they gave me these flowers but I do know that it happened so fast that I was left holding this pot of flowers, wondering what to do. So I decided to head back up to my friend's room. As I entered, my friend sat straight up in his bed and reached for one of the flowers, broke it off and clutched it to him.

I was not present when he died but my mother told me later that he never let that flower far from his sight even as he took his last breath. He had been an avid gardener when he was a younger man and this particular flower, I learned, had been his favourite. I do not even remember the type of flower now but I do believe that my friend had asked God to send him this flower as a sign.'

These are moments that deepen faith and insight, in which time is invited to answer questions, but never to the extent that the questions are taken away.

12

ALL MY RELATIONS

She has the same name as the woman Jesus shared his true purpose with before anyone else. It was her strength and generosity that Christ responded to. She was not afraid to argue with him as well as venerate.

Biblical Martha's sense of purpose, coupled with faith and hospitality, is reflected in the direct, warm tones and giving of Donegal Martha. She is working hard to open a new health food store. Every day she sees herons and feels that their message is to pay close attention to detail. As I listen to her speak we are sharing a lot of connections: both of us have worked as healthcare assistants to the elderly, both have an affinity with herons and both have a Mateus Rosé story. Hers involves giving a bottle of it to her father on the eve of his perfect death, which he drank on the day of his perfect death. Mine involves getting drunk for the first time in the living quarters of a home for ex-servicemen, where I worked, and running through the corridors shouting at the top of my voice: 'You don't do enough for these soldiers. You don't treat them as men.' The night watchman and my house mate, Caroline, got me to bed before I lost my job.

Martha called to her parents' house on the eve of her father's birthday, a Sunday, to spend it with him. She brought her four children:

'He was a wonderful grandfather, played with the children, putting squirty cream in their mouths when my back was turned. I'd brought it for a flan I was going to make up for him as a cake. He had had a heart condition for many years, fifteen of them, and he was in that wonderful period just before death that many get, which is just like a candle before the wick finally burns through.'

I know exactly what she means. I lit a candle every night for my partner's safe return to his family, when he moved back to the UK without us. I also prayed to and for his recently deceased father, feeling he was the only one who could understand his son's pain and distance. One night the candle flared for one last burst of light and lit up the entire room.

That burst of light, in Martha's father, brought him to have a long telephone conversation with his son, despite the fact that he hated the phone and would happily have lived without one. He also enjoyed a renewed sense of love with his wife who, as Martha recalls, was suffering from carer's fatigue at this point. He had a visit from his other daughter. And he died on his birthday. As Martha puts it:

'He and Mum enjoyed a lovely lunch and the bottle of Mateus Rosé I had brought for him the previous day. Then he went out to his studio to work on his painting, which he finished. On his way back to the house, he had a heart attack right at the front door. My mother, who was in the house, heard the phone ring and she distinctly heard him say: "That bloody phone; you always answer it." She was on the phone for twenty minutes and when she came off it she thought she ought to see what was keeping him so long down at the studio. He was dead outside the front door and had been for at least a half an hour. So his spirit got stroppy with the phone ringing as much as he did in his physical body!

'They had planned how they were to be buried long before he died so we just got on with what had been agreed with my father: he wanted to buried in his orchard. The ceremony and situation were both powerful and fitting for a life and a passion for landscape as he had.

Martha later trained as a healthcare assistant to the elderly:

'I gained a deeper understanding of the process of growing old and imminent death and a respect for the process of life, how fragile it is.'

I wrote a novel with some measure of my experience in the same kind of work in it. The measure of my Mateus Rosé experience was also in that time.

Talking to this woman I experience what I have come to appreciate elsewhere on this journey, a sense of connection that goes beyond conversation and enquiry into shared experience. The garden beyond words, where higher selves meet and acquaint.

Sometimes the words themselves are a connection. She feels the connections too, when I ask her to spell out: '*Duw cariad Yw*' – 'God is love' in Welsh – quoted by one of her fellow Bible-study students in a Methodist chapel every Sunday:

'The rest of us had to learn and perfect a psalm perfectly. We were so envious she got away with this each week. But now the words are in my mind.' I respond to them too. She then tells me she has a lovely picture of her grandparents, whom her mother was estranged from and whom she barely knew, at their local church. Written on the wall of the church, behind them, is, '*Duw cariad Yw*'. Martha knows her grandparents now through a key moment, given to her by her younger son in a childhood drawing.

'He's fourteen now and questions whether there is a God. When he was born he came with a whole contingent; the house was full of wonderful moment and movements. It was an incredible, unique and indescribable time. There was peace in our home because everyone was at peace. His guides were so strong they affected us all.

'When he was five my grandmother, Nora, whom he had only met once, was getting ready to die. She was ninety-two and had buried her husband in the previous year. For the last ten years of their lives my mother had reconciled with her parents, so I had grandparents for the first time. Both of them were still alive when we visited but they were in a nursing home and senility had set in.'

Martha's grandmother was in Wales, not an easy journey from Donegal, so there was no opportunity for her to go to her deathbed with four young children. Her mother kept her informed on the phone and told her: 'It's close now. It's just a matter of waiting for when.'

Martha went upstairs after the call to find her five-year-old son drawing a picture: 'This is Grandma, sitting on her chair. Grandpa is in the sky and this is him coming to collect her.' While he was drawing the picture and explaining it to his mother, his great-grandmother passed away.

'I still have that picture in my box of treasures. My grandparents spoke to me through my little boy and my eyes were opened to ancestral connection. Whether you know one another physically or not, you are connected. You are part of the web of life.'

Ancestral connections are often dismissed in our culture but not in most parts of the world and in most ways of living. We are connected by blood and history to the generations before and we carry that history without even realising it. For every cell of conscious memory there are forty-eight subconscious cells working and it's there the lineage is placed: in memories, in dispositions and expressions our great-grandparents would have used. It's for this reason some Native Americans use the phrase: 'All my relations'.

It's the strength of this realisation, coupled with her decision to live her life truthfully, that has helped Martha through the worst pain of her life. Ironically it was also the decision to live according to her spiritual principles that caused the pain she describes as a death without a body, a death of a relationship.

Martha's life is changing. In 1999, the year of her father's perfect death, she was working nights in a chipper to supplement the family income for herself and four young children. Now she is separated, living differently, embarking on a new career and her children, all in their teenage years, no longer require her constant care. It is clear how maternal she is, how strong she is in letting them become, as Kahlil Gibran puts it: 'the product of life's longing for itself'. She has, over the past nine years, found a spiritual expression that has changed her utterly and her circumstances with it.

Nine years ago she was working as a teller in the local credit union when a flyer for an angel workshop was placed in her hand:

'We used to get notices for all sorts of things but when I saw this one, I was unequivocal in my desire to go to it. I went, not really knowing what it was about or what to expect. The woman who was facilitating, her personality and style of presentation really appealed to me. She was softly spoken and in tune; she also had a telepathic connection with me. She led us on a guided meditation to meet our guardian angel. The first name that came to me was Gabriel. Immediately I rejected this, inside myself, thinking there was no way a super-duper archangel would come in for someone like me. But the facilitator picked up on this and said, "Don't be surprised if it's an archangel's name."

'Then I had the sense of another angel, who was my guardian. Her name wouldn't come to me but I could define the presence. The facilitator told us that if the name didn't come to us now, it would somehow come to us later. It would keep coming up. In the following days a friend called round with a mini-rose plant, I had a wrong number for someone looking for Rose and I fell into a dog-rose bush. Angels have a sense of humour. I decided then my other angelic guide was Rose.

'From then I went on to do another angel workshop with my facilitator, to train in Reiki and Seichim, a form of energy healing using Egyptian methods and symbolism. It's very feminine compared to the Tibetan Reiki form.'

During her training Martha found herself moving on all levels. She had married and had her children young, so this part of her life, it appears from how I encounter her, was about self-identity and finding the way to her own formation as individual and spirit. A cyst in her sinus cavity caused aggravation and she had surgery to remove it. As she began to breathe more easily, her mind also was clearing:

'Healing comes in all guises and, as I came closer to my own truth, I saw it was not just about angels but about our ancestors, about the signs nature offers. My father was a landscape painter and my mother is an herbalist and author. They took the time to acquaint us with nature and we grew up in rural Wales and Donegal, so I haven't lived divorced from nature and the seasons.'

But she did decide that her marriage was not fulfilling and she got the courage and strength to leave: 'In the past five years particularly, I have walked the walk. I have had to put all my spiritual ideals into practice. Leaving my husband was definitely the right thing to do. I prayed and prayed that it would be the right thing for everybody, himself and the children too. Sadly the aftermath of the separation has meant I am now estranged from my elder son. He was fourteen at the time of the split.'

Martha is aware that teenage decision-making is very black-and-white; she also knows that what made spiritual sense for her was not something her son could accept or reason with. Her actions were unforgivable to him. She found this a common response in people she encountered outside the family:

'There is horrendous shame in being estranged from your own offspring. The immediate reaction of many people is, "What did you do? You must have been awful to your child." For a long time I was doing the same to myself, thinking of all the things I had done wrong and should have done better. I felt as horrendous as the shame I experienced in the reaction of others. There was no peace in my heart and no peace in my son's. I tried everything until I realised that I could do nothing.'

Again she turned to her spiritual guides and practice for support, along with a memory she has of him, shortly after his birth:

'What I experienced that night with my son as an infant on my lap was what I describe as a 'recognition of each other's souls'. The memory of that moment is what reminds me that on a higher level, away from all this human stuff, we know and love each other.

'I asked for help, prayed for help and in doing so handed the situation over to my angels and guides. This led me to a place where I could "let go" and it was shortly after this that I discovered the estranged stories site. I wrote a blog of my situation and progress and received tremendous empathy, support and advice from my "cyber angels" there until I got to a point where I could honestly declare, "It is what it is." And that became my mantra!'

The bigger picture is one her estranged grandparents have helped her with. Martha now makes a direct correlation between the drawing her younger son gave her and the spiritual help she is receiving to deal with her elder son's alienation and absence:

'They knew the agony of a lost child. My mother. And the agony of not seeing their grandchildren grow up. Their spirit visited me through my own son and now I've lost one. But they taught me that when families are estranged, spirit transcends all the years of not knowing one another.'

I get the impression she is not persuading herself. She is philosophical in her loss and has come out of the dark place where the wrench was too much to bear. This way is seeing herself and her son in the vast design, contracted to teach other lessons which may have value in future lifetimes, or when this one ends and goes to wherever afterlife is:

'I think of the macaroni necklace we used to make as children. I see my lifetime as one piece of dried macaroni on a string and my spirit as the string. I think when this piece is threaded and my son's piece is threaded, we might emerge from the tunnel and say to each other something of the value we got from our experience of each other.'

She uses another image of them having tea and biscuits and discussing their contract. I visualise a *Brief Encounter* platform café serving tea from a Burco and good scones. Mother and son at a table, threading macaroni on their strings:

'I'll say to him, "Thanks for the lesson in how to handle grief." Hopefully he will say, "Thanks for the lesson in dealing with my anger." My spirituality tells me this lifetime of ours is a blink of an eye. He may come around. He may never come around. He may come around on my deathbed. He may come around next week. I can't hang my "happiness' or "contentment" on whether he is in my life or not…He may never accept what I did. I have to live my life and accept his choice not to be a part of it.'

She knows her spiritual development caused her marriage to end and her son to leave her side and also that it gave her the will to keep going towards her own self and making.

'I have no way forward except acceptance. The crack in the door I leave open is a card at Christmas and his birthday saying, "Thinking of you, as ever."

13

CALLING ALL ANGELS

Angelic Companions is a small shop off Main Street in Gorey, run by Margaret, a woman who was in the grocery trade all her life. A sudden urge to change her life brought her to an uncharacteristic decision: to ignore her pragmatic, analytical instincts and resign. It wasn't just a job but living accommodation she was giving up. Three months working in a friend's angel shop showed her that work was not always about stress.

A sign outside the door says: 'Please feel free to come in and browse.' There is no obligation to buy. This lack of obligation means that the day I visited, Margaret was busy, not just selling but talking. When people visit an angel shop they're not just buying products, they're looking for emblems and inspiration. They're looking, some of them, to share their story. I can't think of another shop where you would reveal to the person behind the counter that your son is going through exam stress and needs something to take away the anxiety. A mother of another son, who is obviously an exam student too, is picking a dream catcher for him. He asked her to go and get it for him. This reminds me of a friend of mine whose twenty-something son went to purchase her a gift for Mother's Day from an angel shop:

'It was nearly as embarrassing for him as going into a sex shop,' she laughed at the time. 'He feels things. But he thinks it's a bit foolish to be seen to feel them.'

Margaret gives me free rein to browse and it isn't long before I realise something. The angel items, with the exception of bronzes, are all female. Even the males are androgynous but the majority of the angelic figures are female. Her shop is laid out in sections: free spirit, which features things like salt and pepper shakers in VW camper style, world music CDs and travelling totems. Then there are items for the dragon followers. In the central aisle there is a variety of butterfly emblems:

'The butterfly is so symbolic of our life here. Pupa, chrysalis, birth and death. They're also the funeral followers. Even at a winter funeral you'll often spot a butterfly.'

I think of Moira, the woman who has nursed at both ends of life, who shares her experiences of this in 'The Blue Love', who was followed by a butterfly at the funeral of her sister and had one hibernating for months in the room where her father died.

I think of the Irish saying: 'Life is the sigh between two mysteries.'

Two women come into the shop: they seem to be regulars, as they call Margaret by name.

'I want a Buddha daddy for the Buddha baby I bought,' one of them grins. Their faces are lined but their eyes shine. They look like women who have seen the two days and come out on the side of smiling. They're beautiful in the truth of their friendship and where it has brought them. One buys the other incense sticks. They discuss something with Margaret and she recommends Bach Rescue Remedy.

'I only ever took it once and it got me through my driving test,' one of them says.

It's not a shop, it's a meeting place in which there are things for sale. I'm thinking of an email which I received from a member of the male clergy: 'I am not a fan of new-age thinking because it is inimical to Christian belief. As a result I do not feel motivated to say anything that might be quoted in such a context. The title of your book intimates that it might be new age in its general orientation.'

Is it 'new age' to see two women in a shop gaining half an hour of solace from the purchase of three euros worth of incense sticks and a good chat with the woman behind the counter serving them? The thing that critics argue about in relation to the explosion of angel shops is their commercialism. But any market, including the soul-driven one, relies on supply and demand. Why are angel shops springing up all over the country? The need of the people who visit them might not be considered well-defined, or might be considered too simplistic by those who live by religious tradition.

'The people coming in here might previously have gone to a priest or rector for advice,' Margaret says. 'Because of what's gone on in the last few years in the church, people are looking for something without necessarily going to a priest for it or a clergyman or whatever. Lots of lovely people out there still, lots of genuine people. Everyone is so hurt that they're looking for something that the church is not providing for them at the moment.'

Margaret, who meets people in search of emblems and talismans every day of her working life, has lots of beautiful things. It's an issue of personal pride with her. But it's also an issue that there should be something for every person and every pocket:

'Browsing is all I ever did in shops when my children were growing up. If you have a euro you'll find something here. And if you don't have a euro you'll find a bit of peace. I love coming to work. After years in retail I finally believe in what I'm selling. For the past year, since the shop opened, I wake up and look forward to the day. Everyone should have that feeling about work. I found it only after a lifetime.'

'I often think people come in to calm down, because you have the music and you have the bits and pieces. That's what I find with people. Especially if someone is going through grief or bereavement or illness. Quieter days in here they could talk for an hour or two. They want to go out feeling that bit better. If you want to talk that's what it's all about.

'This is spirituality without the religion.'

Talk is free. We all need it. The words of the Jane Siberry song come back to me, the tape that Mary T. dances to around her kitchen when she's making those fabulous cookies: 'Walk me through this world/ Don't leave me alone.'

Jim is a priest and psychotherapist who encourages his parishioners to talk to him, not hear from him. His Sunday mass attracts people from miles around. He fills his churches with music and often invites people to share their own life reflections at mass. His family services attract a wide range of people who want to have an input. He also runs regular groups to discuss family issues in a safe setting, for people to offer one another the counselling they would otherwise have to pay for. It's his view that diocesan priests would be better served by training in human development and psychotherapy more than philosophy. He is in touch with the humanity of his parish, rather than being distant from it:

'It's more grounded. It's what seminarians need to know. It's what parishioners need.'

What does he think of the visual depictions of angels?

'I don't know, I haven't really formulated my own thinking on that except that, in one sense of a visitation of an angel I had, the first thing I noticed was that he didn't have wings. I was wondering about this afterwards. I found that art that has placed wings on angels; yet, people who talk about angels manifesting themselves to them often talk about there being no wings.

'I had an experience myself and I wondered if there was an angel involved. I'm not so sure. I was travelling very early one Saturday morning. I was coming up to quite a severe bend and I heard a very strong whisper saying, "Stop, stop, stop." I slowed down and pulled in to the side and stopped and waited. Within seconds a car careered around the corner on the wrong side. The occupant was obviously asleep. He skidded across, narrowly missed me, seemed to wake up as he hit the ditch and got back on to the road without having a crash. I look back at that: was it the whisper of an angel? 'I can't say but I think it was.

I look back at other experiences in my life and there have been a lot of encounters. One of the most remarkable goes back about seven years ago. I was working with somebody in counselling. I became very aware that there was something I wasn't getting to the root of. There was a behaviour pattern that just wasn't making sense and I was puzzled by it. Then I went on retreat. The day I started the retreat, I got word that this girl had been diagnosed with a serious brain tumour.

'That evening, I went to the chapel, I spent a couple of hours in prayer bringing her before the Lord. Went back to my room, spent another hour in prayer. And then, this is the only way I can describe it, out of the blue, I wasn't thinking of anything, simply praying, but suddenly there was a presence in the room. Instinctively, I knew it was the presence of an angel, it was a presence from another world. A magnificent beam of light. He didn't have wings, it wasn't that kind of presence. A warm, benign, loving presence.

'It was as if you had all the worries of the world on your shoulders and just his presence would suddenly lift everything. That kind of sense, an incredible peace. It wasn't that I could reach out and touch him. I could put my hand through him, yet he was so strong I could see all the features. I was completely overcome by this. I cried, I cried just in awe of this magnificent creature in front of me.'

What the presence then went on to show Jim was quite specific, that the young woman's life was now in the balance, as surgeons went to work.

'The next morning I woke up, mulling over this experience. I went for a walk on the beach at about 7.30 and suddenly he appeared again. Again, no words: there was no actual communication, yet there was communication. It was a strange experience in that way. I looked at his face and the face was one of complete satisfaction. His face communicated, "Job done, everything is fine."

'I rang the mother, who was by the daughter's bedside. Her daughter had been afraid to go to sleep that night because she was afraid it might be her last on this earth. But she'd had the most restful sleep. I was sure that everything was a success and so it was. She took a while to come to full recovery but she did and she's since got married and got on with her life. Everything was fine.'

Jim has kept this aspect of his spirituality, despite what he describes as the seminary's attempts to remove it:

'Our religious training has pushed us away from the experience of God, which is very strange. We have been taught to cultivate our heads and to identify with our thoughts and we've been taught to distrust anything of the deeper person.

'The definition of the human person for so long, since the time of Descartes, was that the human being is a rational animal. We've been trained to identify with thinking and anything that wasn't thought was viewed with suspicion. I think we're much more specks of intellect on the seas of emotion. I prefer that kind of definition:

that there's so much more to us than meets the eye.

'I think there is a profound spiritual awakening taking place among people today at grass-roots level and more and more people are talking about these experiences. But not necessarily within institutional religion. There is a suspicion of religious experiences within institutional religion that is very strange, whereas people who maybe never go to church are much more at home talking about spiritual matters now than people who may be going to church every day of the week. In the seminary all the focus was on intellect: very little on heart, on emotion, on soul. We talked years ago about saving souls and we hadn't a clue what souls meant. I think, in reality, that what we are experiencing now is people's souls awakening, and often through negative experiences, the difficult experiences of life, people are coming alive.

'I'd like to mention a scientist of the last century, Teilhard de Chardin, who was a Jesuit. He said that we are not human beings trying to become more spiritual; first of all we are spiritual beings trying to have a human experience. I think God comes to us disguised as our lives and we don't know it.'

How did his psychotherapeutic training assist him; how did it open up his life?

'It made me aware that, in our theology and stuff, we had moved more and more away from the basic message of incarnation. Instead of seeing life as a journey into the embrace of all that it means to be human, we tried to escape, got into the place where we were trying to escape being human and slipping off into a spiritual never-never world. Where we were encouraged to block off the human story, block off the ancestral story, leave behind our emotions and just get on. And if something of that were to come into our lives we were expected to offer it up but there was no chance of integrating it into our lives.'

He tells me about the people he has encountered, how it has come about, individuals professing their faith in their own way.

'I travel a good bit giving seminars in different parts of the country. What I see is that there is a spiritual awakening taking place in people's lives but it's taking place in people who are in some way embracing their human reality, people who have grappled with core issues in their life: issues like grief, issues like self-esteem, issues all relating to human development. Out of that, then, there's a kind of spiritual awakening coming in.

'It's as if when we fully embrace our humanness we discover our spiritual nature. Then they say that they go to church: they often go to church and they find that where they're at on their journey is not being met. The authentic spiritual journey is a journey into the embrace all that it means to be human.'

What does Jim think an angelic journey comprises?

'A journey into the acceptance of all that can seem quite un-acceptable. I must have the courage to face my human story: share something of my own vulnerabilities and weaknesses and mistakes. In that process, there is intimacy.'

He rejects the chintzy portrayal of angelicism as a panacea for those who are looking for light without any recognition of the deep and dark:

'It's frothy. It lacks body. It doesn't have the depth. I think the kind of thing I would always be looking for is: does it help me to be more grounded in my humanness? It's in the embrace of what it means to be human that we discover or rediscover our core spiritual nature.'

How does one develop the courage to take the messages that arrive in our hearts unbidden?

'Live out of that deeper place.'

Regardless of consequence?

'Oh, to risk is to live. It's only by taking the risk. But to follow spirit in life, surely, is the way that leads to life.'

How do you know you are arriving at a good place spiritually?

'If you follow the deeper self, follow the deeper intuition, you go beyond the place of having to know whether it's right or wrong. Just follow it and trust that if it's right, it'll be confirmed and if it's wrong you'll be put on a different path. But you must move, you have to be prepared to take the risks. The only way you can steer a car is when it's moving. So often, we'll sit still, in fear, twisting the steering wheel, thinking: "Should I go this way, should I go that way?" But the car doesn't move. Start moving in a particular direction and you are allowing yourself to be directed. Now this might mean taking the risks. Follow the intuition and doing the thing, that deeper hunch, if you like. If you follow that, it's amazing then what happens or what can open up.'

I think about this a lot afterwards. Everyone I speak to is saying the same thing in a different way. Make new journeys, discoveries, stories and histories, much like our ancients did, much like the future generations will. Your life becomes an expression of who you are, in the given days. Your life is not about producing results; it's about bearing fruit. The role of the angel is to mediate this at some level. Whether your angel is your inner voice or a statue in your living room or the turn of a card, you have your own way. Listening is an act.

Jim has words to say on listening:

'The word listen and the word silent are composed of the same letters. Same word, same letters, same number of letters in each. The importance of being able to give yourself time for silence in life is to give yourself the ability to listen.'

Margaret listens each day to the human stories; observes and assists the human search for spirit. Jim does the same. They are working in different ways, at different ends of the spiritual spectrum, but they are working with the same silence.

14

The Crone Returns

Recently she was on what she anticipates as being her last trip to Canada, to say goodbye to the place that was home for most of her life. At a gathering of hundreds, she was asked to give her blessing to them, as the oldest attending.

'The crone is returning,' Bríd smiles, in writing. 'Not a minute too soon. 'While historians are trying to sift out the fragments and put them together, I have personally attended several workshops on crone spirituality, as well as given them, over the past decades. We are hearing more and more stories from older women who are meeting and naming their situations, claiming their power and making themselves heard.

'The modern crone's voice is raised to challenge and heal this fragmented world. I am glad that I have lived to see this day and can add my voice to those of my sister crones, for the sake of ourselves and generations to come.

'Where do I get the kind of energy that this work is calling on? I believe it comes from the *anam cara* tradition. Go off and don't eat until you get a soul friend, because anyone without a soul friend is a body without a head.

'For some years now I have been a spiritual guide in the Celtic tradition of *anam cara*. To be a soul friend…is to walk with another in a non-judgemental way, putting that person in touch with his or her own story, his or her own voice, and encouraging them to trust it.'

As the oldest contributor to this book Bríd has blessed it. She makes me want to grow old, to live my long days. There is a liberation call for ageing women in her words but there is also pain in this message:

'Crones have long memories but in so many ways our memories need to be healed. We are of a generation who are recovering our voices…Crones are mentors if we live our lives honestly and are not afraid to share our wisdom. I took many decades to find meaning in my "religious" background. Now it feels as if I have come full circle.'

Bríd's life is an example to me of how to handle my goodbyes. She has had so many of them. I read her words and I feel the fear flood out of my pores. There is a point at which faith puts you in front a mirror and says, 'Accept.'

Once I interviewed Julie Christie, who was turning fifty. At one point she tore herself on the truth and the pain ripped through her voice: 'Why did I not know I was beautiful? Why did I not just go out there and love it?'

I understand now. Women my own age and younger discuss botox as if it is a necessary evil. In an age when we are supposed to be more free, we are more chained, men and women, to our appearances, to endurance on treadmills, machines that make us run faster and take us nowhere. Even post-partum figures are denied us. We must emerge as if we never carried children or laboured. Our bodies are asked to appear as if life never intruded or put demands on them. Fame is the new cathedral. The red carpet is Jacob's ladder, the ascending and the descending travel on it, denying life. Celluloid angels. As if they were beyond sorrow, ageing and death. To keep immortal they employ surgeons to deal with the skin with scalpels and injections, shock treatments and animal fats. But they look like angels. And we revere them. Our Cleopatras. Their lives are rarely as beautiful as their roles. Their sorrows and decline are pitiful. But when these human butterflies hold the ephemeral for those flash-lit seconds, it's heaven on earth.

Then age begins. And fear rises.

Ageing is a spiritual journey. It is a gift that we give over our youthful appearance to an increase in wisdom. Joy and happiness are indicators of balance. We swap bikini stomachs for wise eyes. We swap toned muscles for children's voices in our homes.

Until today.

Where is the place for the older and wiser? Who is listening to them? I wanted to find a woman who had expertise in the area of spirituality and ageing. I found Bríd, in her eighty-eighth year. She is close to six feet tall and walks tall, proud, fluid, everywhere. She is Mary T.'s friend and was the chief celebrant of her marriage:

'Even though there were three priests at the small and intimate event, Bríd was the presiding spirit and inspiration for much of the ceremony.'

Bríd, as one of her gifts, has expertise in the area of spirituality of the older woman. She was born by a river and all her awareness, it seems, has come from observances made close to water. She sees time and its effect on soul as a river path. The closer we are to end the richer we are. She is in her delta years, about to meet the open sea.

She was born during the Civil War in an inner room protected from bullets. Each window in her house was filled with bags of feathers. They were close to the river in her native New Ross and a regular target during gun battles.

Her mother died of cancer when she had just turned fifteen:

'I came across a book in Canada called *Motherless Daughters*. One contributor wrote about her mother dying when she was the same age as me but she never got over it. Without doubt the loss of the mother at a young age has many repercussions in later years. The circumstances leading up to and around my mother's death are as vivid as if they happened yesterday.'

Her mother and father's quiet approach to spirituality governed her own, particularly her mother's:

'Many decades have passed yet her memory is green within me. My own spiritual journey has been influenced by her love of creation and music and by her deep spiritual core, which brought out her humanity to all and sundry. There are many questions left un-answered for me although I feel, too, that I have tried to live some aspects of my life that were denied by her early death. Above all I learned the legacy of friendship, a legacy beyond price.'

Her words foreshadow those of Donagh in the next chapter.

'I felt very definitely that I had to follow Christ wherever he led.'

She joined an order that sent its nuns anywhere in the world but their home country. She came home to Ireland to study in UCD but her life was going to be far away. 'I didn't know it then.' It was 1941, January, when she stepped on to the mail boat at Dún Laoghaire.

'I remember wishing Hitler would come and bomb it I was so seasick.'

When it docked she was in rationed Britain. Her novitiate overlooked the English Channel and their view was of a lookout with a gunner and his machine gun at the ready. The sounds of the war for Bríd were an air-raid sirens, bombers and gunfire. And involvement was a gas mask and chain-gang duties digging out the chalk ground to build the order's air raid shelter. No newspapers, no outside connection. In July 1941 she said goodbye to her long hair. Her head was shaved. She asked for a curl of it to be sent home to her sister.

'Fifty years later, when I was sorting out her things after her death, I found it.'

The order decided to send her to Canada and sent her home to say her goodbyes to her family. It was as if her soul had always known where she was to be sent:

'The strange thing was that my favourite country in Geography at school had been Canada. I was to join a small community that was opening a house and boarding school in Ontario, in small village on the Madawaska River. The names intrigued me.'

This was 1948. Half a century later, exactly, Bríd returned to Ireland a lay person, to rejoin the family she had said goodbye to.

'I was in the religious life for close to thirty-three years. I am the same length out of it now that I was in it. I am eighty-seven years of age now. I love to walk and be alive and I'm grateful to the spirit all around us that I can still do that and be there for the people who need me.'

I ask Bríd about her decision to leave the convent. To have got to that stage of life and practice, to decide it was no longer for her, must have been a terrible blow:

'It was and it wasn't. I became so alive through the decision and the things that transpired out of it. It was a journey I had to make. I also was going to meetings, open meetings, where my order was having to examine the way it did things and I saw the change would not be enough. I had some sisters in the convent who were of the same mind. I had to be very careful not to influence them in my decision to leave, as I was their "superior". She says this with a wry smile. Her faith now is not in hierarchical practice but in spiritual communion:

'I was working in this amazing place in Toronto, with a French priest, a high-rise area with people from sixty-two different countries. I helped them to learn how to run a community. It meant being involved with them right from baptism to last rites.

'You live by what you believe and that keeps changing. I came home to Ireland and found nothing had changed.'

Instead of being disillusioned by this, Bríd works quietly to bring life into her church and her people.

'Love one another as I have loved you, Christ is about that. He worked with the poor and the powerless more than any other grouping. It's the same now as it was in his time. You have the group that wants to keep control all the time and then you have the people who are on the bottom, the suffering, the ones not listened to.

What does she believe God to be? What does she believe the messages of God are?

'I don't think like that. I don't think in terms of messages. I see God as all-being. We are part of that being. Each person is of God, portrays something of God, if they're trying to live as well as they can, positively, and connected with everything. Love, compassion and mercy. They are all part of the word of Christ, which becomes part of you when you try to live it. You see the connection between all creation and everything that happens.

'I don't see magic as such. I see working at it and being open to whatever happens. Being really open to what happens and connecting with it as far as you can. If you go back to love and justice and compassion they are the basics of life. We're called to them all the time. Any concern we express for a fellow human.'

She has noticed, through her years, that women tend to waste themselves, in the name of spirituality, instead of building themselves up. It's one of her important messages to women growing older:

'I have to watch myself too that I don't go so far that I lose myself entirely in care. You have this issue with your mothering. Sometimes we can care too much. I need replenishing. Awareness means being in touch with yourself, your own being, and in that becoming aware of others.'

A vital part of ageing is being more aware of death:

'I see it as part of life. Because my mother died when I was fifteen, I was very much aware of it. I've had a conscious awareness of death throughout my life.'

Soul friends mirror each other. When Bríd supported Mary T.'s initiatives and magazine, she was called to her mother house, where her novitiate had begun, to be questioned on her actions.

'During that time I was aware of fear: how easy it is to change your intentions through fear. But also I became aware of the power of prayer. I remember thinking that my ordeal reminded me of how Jesus must have felt at Gethsemane.

'When the sessions finally ended I was weak as a rag. But I had a strong feeling that no matter what happened I had to hold on to my belief. I was then given a week to go to Ireland to see my family. When Peg, my sister, saw me she exclaimed: "What have they done to you?" She put me to bed and waited on me hand and foot for days.'

On the last day of 1973, a cold day, just like the day she had entered the convent, she spent a day by the lake: 'In reflection and prayer about my journey. At the end I calmly decided that the time had come to leave.

'Among other things I began to work as supervisor to students for ministry, both clerical and lay, in Toronto School of Theology. I think these were the ten best years of my life. There was a great variety of field placements: parishes, jails, hospitals, detox centres, schools, nursing homes, places where prostitutes were looked after and many more. It was interesting to supervise the students in the field and see how they did. I was learning myself all the time…I had become interested in Celtic spirituality and in 1992 came back to Dublin to do a course in this.'

Bríd is a Brigid, a woman of the old times before the fall of magic. She has no time for magic yet her presence is magical. Being in her company it is clear that her interest, and gift, is in drawing others out, remaining honest and loving towards them. I feel myself being listened to, being taken on in full. I am telling her something I haven't said to anyone else on the angel journey: 'This book is about looking for my identity. I am questioning my approach to my life and my spirit.'

'There is a risk in any life undertaking, a risk of commitment,' Bríd explains.

The older we get, the more risks we may meet. Bríd's awareness of this has encouraged her to develop her natural inclination to journey with others on their quest. This desire, to be a soul friend, has brought the magic of friendship into her life. Bríd is surrounded by friends, making new ones all the time, by refusing to be cut off from life and the wisdoms. She closes the garden gate as I leave, waves me goodbye, gives me the wonderful, the simple message: 'Enjoy your life.'

15

Angel of Friendliness

I ring the doorbell of the Dominican Retreat Centre in Tallaght, where I have arranged to talk to Donagh, a priest, potter, philosopher and writer who, among other things, has lived in a tent and in a Zen monastery in the Catskill mountains.

I know the grounds of the centre and old Tallaght village well. In 1985 I was selling door-to-door here, in shoes with worn heels and scuffed toes. I walked with a perpetual question in my mind, waiting for the results, praying to the God of the CAO and the points race.

Life is a circle. I have a powerful sense of seeing how far I have come, not just on this journey but on the road in general. I have never stopped being the thin girl who was afraid of everything, especially herself, and dismissed the hearts of others, especially her own.

You can revisit yourself in places. I have the same feeling in my stomach as I had then. When I lay eyes on Donagh I feel the powerful experience of kindred. He is kind, bearded and looks like an old English teacher of mine, Denstone, who was an ex-Dominican and an angel I forgot. Years later I learned he had written to another ex-Dominican, David Rice, to suggest me as a suitable candidate for the gold-dust journalism course he ran at DIT, and which I got on to, thanks to prayer (mine and my family's) and intervention (Denstone's).

By the time I learned this, Denstone was dead. He had also written to congratulate me on my career and in my excuse for busyness, I never replied. I was back from London for a few days; he had written to my home address. The letter did not mention how much of an instrument he had been in my future. I never imagined he would have done this. I had no concept of anyone believing in me or of mentors. I felt entirely alone, inside a thin frame, making bargains with God. I stood in the porch of the church beside the retreat centre and thought my future would never come.

Now it's my past.

Life is circle.

Never forget your angels.

Donagh shows me into his office, then vanishes on a message, whether it is angelic or not. I find I am crying tears of relief and I really don't know why. But my spirit already knows: this is the last of the synchronicities. This is the journey's end.

Angel Journey, a book of conversations about spirit with others and myself, with people from all persuasions, with those who have had spiritual encounters beyond my own and with my own consternation at my lack of faith. A journey in which I made new and deep friendships and found new spiritual direction.

Donagh says, on his return: 'All my life has been a conversation.'

I realise this is the end. The book did not rest and now it seems to. Today I meet myself as a much younger woman. And I meet a man with whom I have a deep connection, just about to be realised. Denstone, if you are an angel, read this now. You were kind to me, and you gave me a message that I was more than myself. You died without my thanks and this is the only place I have to thank you now. Today I meet another who has memories of you.

I say, 'You remind me of my old English teacher. He's the reason I became a writer. Denstone.'

'Well, that's funny. He's the reason I became a priest.'

I was seventeen when Denstone came to my assistance, to give my life direction. Donagh was sixteen:

'I met Denstone by chance in Cork city one day fifty years ago. I had spent a couple of years as an internee in a normal grim boarding school where the enforcers wore black and I was immediately struck by Denstone's cream habit. At some unconscious level I may have felt that he was as different from those others as day from night. As he spoke, and especially as he listened, I realised that he was. I was sixteen but he treated me with courtesy and respect. That half-hour conversation led me some years later to become a Dominican myself.

'My life has been a continual conversation: with confrères, with places, with books, with people everywhere, with God; part of that conversation is now through the internet. I have a lot of reasons to be grateful to Denstone. People remember him as a man who talked to everyone. Of course lots of us talk to everyone, but what makes people remember that unrelentingly friendly man is that he also listened.'

As I listen to Donagh, I come back to Jim, the diocesan priest in 'Calling All Angels'. He told me about the words 'listen' and 'silent' falling into the same frame. Listening to Donagh I am silent to the memory of Denstone, feeling his impression inscribed on our lives. Within minutes we discover another piece of common ground: comic strips. He is a Donald Duck fan and learned Norwegian through reading the strips in that language:

'I'm happy to speak well of my really good teachers. I can't understand why people spend small fortunes on language courses when Donald Duck could do a much better job with two shakes of his tail. He can teach every language. In Rome a woman looked at me curiously when I bought some volumes of Donald but her face lit up with appreciation when I told her he was my language professor. I don't know why school libraries in Ireland aren't full of him. He would make a brilliant teacher of Irish. And students would readily identify with him: he's nearly always in big trouble.'

As is anyone on the road less travelled. As is Calvin. I am a Calvin and Hobbes fan. There is so much wisdom in a cartoon. Calvin, aged six, turns to his tiger Hobbes, who comes alive when adults are not present, and says, 'Sometimes I think the surest sign that intelligent life exists elsewhere in the universe is that none of it has tried to contact us.'

If you are open to life, you will get signs. You will be like Calvin and Donald, always in trouble, you will be contacted. Your tiger will come alive.

Donagh is giving me his take on his own life and on angels in it:

'I'm not used to talking much about myself but I think faith is never a solitary walk. The journey begins long before we are born and we have countless companions along the way, some living, some long dead. Call them angels, if you will: messengers of God. Sometimes when I hear people's horror stories I feel something close to guilt that my own parents were so gentle, so uncomplicated and so good. I've been luckier than I deserve to be. I've never been able to project blame on them that I am not a better man. Their lives unfolded in a simpler world than ours, but like everyone they could have found reasons to be hard and bitter – if it was in them. Our parents' lives are a "message" that goes deeper than words. I still keep discovering details of it, though my parents have been dead for many years. They were the real mediators of faith for me and I often think I would have lost or discarded it long ago if it hadn't been for them.

'When I presented myself in 1961 at the Dominican novitiate in Cork, all I had to go on was the memory of a conversation with Denstone, whom I had met near that very building some years earlier, and who was a real gentleman. That seems a narrow base on which to build a future life but isn't that how it always is? "Reasons" are nearly always retrospective; we are led by the heart, whether we call it that or something else. Imagination, maybe.'

What were the mountains for him on his faith journey?

'The mountains? There were many. First there was the struggle to become an adult in a single-sex world. I would have been lost on that mountain if it wasn't for the general friendliness of Dominicans and of a few in particular. Our numbers have always been small, so we really know nothing of the chill of "ecclesiastical life". (That word suggests icebergs to me; it's enough to make me content with mountains.) Also, everything is democratic with us: all our leaders at every level are elected and they come back down the ladder once their term of office comes to an end. We could be described as an egalitarian society (chilly words, too) but a better word would be "brotherly". Of course we have the drawbacks of democracy as well: a concentration of fools can elect a fool or get rid of a good man. It's a system that can often seem inefficient in the short term but it's good in the long run: it shows respect for the individual, whether he's a fool or not.

'If I had to name an angel I would call it Friendliness.

'Soon there was another mountain – an Alp, to be exact. I was suddenly sent to Switzerland to study theology, though I had neither French nor German from school. Doing it will teach you, they said. There I discovered in practice the worldwide nature of the Dominican family. There I also discovered that friendliness isn't always an Irish brand; there are other brands that don't seem like friendliness at the time. Maybe there are cooler angels in the Alps, taking care of us all the same.

'Several years later, starting to teach philosophy in England was a kind of mountain. I have never met the feathered kind of angel but that college had a great number of wonderfully friendly human angels. They were tolerant of my youth and inexperience and my half-digested philosophical patter. Later, after teaching philosophy in Tallaght for five years, I began to experience deserts rather than mountains. Philosophy began to undermine me – which is what philosophy does best when it is laid on a foundation of youth.

'Also, at that time, the 1970s, numerous confrères were abandoning the priesthood and religious life. "The Changes", as Vatican II was called by people like my parents, were not just changes within a game but changes to a different game. I was just about ready to take that path. Then one afternoon I had a visitation from an angel in the form of a confrère, brother, who listened to my outpourings till four am. It caused me to pause and not abandon everything at once. I unfolded my plan for gradual departure to a large-minded superior and he just asked me what I wanted to do. I wanted to train as a potter, I told him. Instead of asking me if I was mad, he picked up the phone and put me in touch with some people in England – whither I went and did just that. He was certainly a good angel, as many others discovered years later when he was master of the order.

'Pottery saved me, in some sense, and I put the other stages of departure on hold. It was just the kind of grounding and practical poetry that I needed.

'Around the same time I began to take a keen interest in Zen, sitting numerous sesshin in different countries. From these twin interests I evolved a kind of retreat/workshop that I have been running for more than thirty years. My angels had to have feet of clay.

And three Zen masters have been angels to me. I could not have survived the deserts without them.'

I skip out of his room a thousand years younger. The Angel of Friendliness has done its work. He tells me he works best when he writes so we agree to correspond by email. I hope it never ends. What I write to ask him, he answers promptly and I have thousands of other questions that I hope to put to him before the end of our time.

This is a glimpse of our correspondence:

Can you please lay out your life for me geographically?
'My friends' eight-year-old daughter asked me recently (eyeing my grey beard), "How old are you?" I said, "I'm two hundred years old." She didn't believe me at first but when I began to tell her what life was like, deep in the country, when I was growing up, she half-believed me and still looks at me with big eyes. People my age have seen two hundred years' worth of change, for sure. When I was her age I lived in a thatched house, with no electricity, no motor-power – almost none of the things we consider essential now. The other day, in the census for 1901, I discovered a great-grandmother born in 1810 – two hundred years ago, as it happens. She lived in the very house where I grew up and I doubt that her life there was very much different from what I knew (except for a few details like the Famine!).

'I told you earlier about meeting Denstone and becoming a Dominican and studying in Switzerland and Italy; teaching in England and in Dublin; then training as a potter. I lived and worked in Ennismore, a retreat centre in Cork, for twelve years: leading retreats and workshops, restoring old buildings, making pottery, sometimes going abroad to give retreats. I was often on the receiving end: I did dozens of courses on all sorts of therapies. It was such great fun. At the end of that time I had a sabbatical year. For part of it I lived in a tent in different places along the west coast of Ireland that held special significance for me, packing up my tent every few weeks and heading off on my battered motorbike to another location. It was the best thing I ever did for myself. I was even inspired to write a book about it: *Take Nothing for the Journey*.

'I became part of a team of four running a renewal centre in

Rome for Dominican men and women from around the world. Meanwhile I taught courses on spirituality and the history of spirituality in various colleges in the city. It was a great time and I made friends from everywhere. In one of those colleges the students came from eighty different countries. Because of knowing so many people from so many places I got invitations to give courses and retreats in lots of countries. I made a list of those countries: it came to about twenty.

'It all came to an end when I was asked to be novice master for the Irish Dominicans. Frankly I was no good at it. At the end of four years I noticed that they didn't ask me to continue! One year we had no novices so I was back on the road. I spent time in a Zen monastery in the Catskill mountains – another of the best things I ever did for myself! I spent a further six years in Cork, writing mostly and doing odd jobs.

'That brings us up almost to the present. I've been director of this retreat centre in Tallaght for the past four years. I'm no good at directing anything but we have an astoundingly good staff. Without them it just wouldn't happen. The challenge is to attract young people (anyone under two hundred years of age) to give their battered nerves a break and experience the peace of this place and the wisdom of contemplation and to lay themselves open to epiphanies of God's presence.

What, for you, is a spiritual message? By this I mean a message which persuades us that we are more than skin and bone? I have a sense they are 'the narrow bases on which we build futures'. This fits with how I have lived.
'I love that phrase, "the narrow bases on which we build futures". I suspect that every future is built on a narrow base: a chance meeting changes your life; even a glance could do it. A friend of mine divides his life into before and after. Before and after what? Before and after a moment, long ago, when he was passing on the stairs and through the door of his parents' bedroom – an inch ajar – he spotted his father praying. The most powerful messages are seldom delivered in words. All the words we use are…just that – used. They are used property.

They describe events as if these events were now over. Words are about the end of something, the summing-up. When something really surprises us we are speechless. When we talk we are arranging things, putting things in their place; we are not being present to what is new. We are dissipating the sense of wonder, not leaving ourselves open to it. As Kavanagh said, "Through a chink too wide there comes in no wonder." A future is built, as you say, on a narrow base – on a moment of wonder.

'I dislike the phrase, "the Christian message". It suggests that it could be written on a piece of paper. It would be great if the word "epiphany" could gain more currency. It means a revelation, a showing. I have a friend whose name is Epifania. Another friend of mine in the Philippines built a mountain retreat centre in which the theme of the artwork in the prayer-room is epiphany – moments of recognition. Moses and the burning bush in *Exodus* 3; the Transfiguration of Jesus in *Matthew* 1…One wall is made of clear glass, giving a breathtaking view over the Batulao hills: it is another epiphany – seeing God in nature.

You can control words – turn them on and off at will. But you can only wait for epiphanies. Many people looking through that clear glass window in Batulao would just see a view but an epiphany is a moment of recognition. Really it's better not even to wait for them; it's better just to forget about them. Then when they come they are fresh. The way to invite epiphanies is to meditate a lot – to leave your mind vulnerable. When you don't bother about them they come in their own way and in their own time. But if you are greedy for them they don't come at all. If they are a product of your own mind they belong to the past. Yes, epiphanies instead of messages…

Without putting you on a spot, do you believe in angels? I respond to your human version, they're mine, but are they more than human?
'A sort of a half-yes! It's a bit less than half if you don't ask me and a bit more than half if you do! They are part of the Christian faith but not a big part. The Greek word for "angel" means "messenger". In the Old Testament the word *mal'ak* (or *mal'akh)* was applied both to human and divine messengers. That kind of ambiguity is still useful!

'But it's interesting to see how they propagate. The more remote God seemed to people, the greater became the need for intermediaries. Certain mighty figures, known later as archangels, make their appearance in the *Book of Daniel*, and the process of naming angels began. Soon there were swarms of them. There was a confusing variety of functions and names – probably because angels were important in popular devotion. All these names have meanings, of course. Michael means "One who is like God", Gabriel means "God is strong", Raphael means "God heals", Daniel means "God judges", and so on. Early Christianity inherited Jewish beliefs about angels but had less interest in them. The angel of the Annunciation has a permanent place in Christian spirituality but the *New Testament* tends if anything to put angels in their place. So in *Hebrews* 1, angels are inferior to the Son; in 1 *Corinthians* 13 the eloquence of angels takes second place to love; and in 1 *Peter* 1 the angels are seen as envying the Christian.

'It seems the spiritual world too abhors a vacuum and now that belief in God is being reprocessed widely, angels are flooding in to fill the vacuum. Modern angels seem to have very sweet natures but in the Jewish world it wasn't always so. Lucifer was an angel of light – his name means "light-bearer" – but he became Satan, prince of darkness; he spanned the spectrum from end to end. But the angels of the new age are all nice and friendly.

'That answer to your question probably doesn't satisfy you, Suzanne. It doesn't satisfy me either. Can we call it work in progress? Someone said recently, with wonderful simplicity, that angels are, "God's thoughts". I could say yes to that.'

Donagh's journey has combined what is best and most silent. It has not confined itself to Christianity or lost Christianity. It has embraced other faith ways, the arts, the wilderness and God's thoughts.

He says so much more in his emails. I wish I had space and time to tell you. I'm continuing to correspond with this angel of friend-liness and through him with myself.

I have a sense that this journey gave me more questions than answers. It certainly gave me powerful memories. It certainly gave me new friends. Like Donagh, my life has taken in many countries. But that's geography. What my heart did was to take in all the encounters, the people, all the energy and the belief to form my convictions.

I believe. In Everything. Just like the story monks of ancient days I am more open to the apocryphal because I have a story soul. The quiet in me likes the inner voice rather than the outer visions others on the journey have had. I have a hammock disposition, committed to the air but staked in the ground.

This was my angel journey. It led me back to a time before I was ever commissioned to write this. It led me back to the beginning of my acceptance that there is more to us, more than us. It led me back to the place where that acceptance began, to all the voices that once touched my condition and still continue to meet it, in my dark moments.

This was my angel journey. I've learned about living energy and teachers arriving when students are ready. I've come to understand the words of the psalm, the words on Carl Jung's gravestone: 'Bidden or not bidden, God is present.' This is written on a plaque by the door of my home.

No one features in this book whom I do not believe. They have varied experiences and varied approaches to that experience. And their shared condition is honesty. The words that came up more than any others? Whisper. Love. Forgiveness. Friendship. Love and forgiveness are a decision.

I have decided to believe in my messages and my epiphanies, tacking and gibing to new horizons. I no longer worry how much of me is in this book. You're in this book. We're all part of the one thing. The same intelligence that flows through you flows through me and through all human beings. We are connected. You can't hurt anyone and not hurt yourself. If you trust, you can be trusted. If you love, you can be loved.

I have decided to come home. Not to a paternalistic God. To the God each and every one of us comprises and contributes towards. To a mother God, a child God, a landscape God, a sky God, a God of elements and endurances.

The people I met were other parts of me and I was other parts of them. They opened tributaries in my mind. Their words, when I return to them, flush out my doubts because of their warmth, life and tears, because of their full admissions. I hear the rush of our time together. The hardest thing about wisdom is what it demands of us. The people of this book met those demands. They reject bitterness and resolve conflicts. I have found in the past two years that every time I am put into conflict with someone, it is so much more about me than them. A successful life is all about how much you can love people, despite the irritations.

We marry everyone we spend time with; we marry our time with theirs. We separate with all the pains when the time ends. They become memories. The more love you have in your memories the happier your condition, the more you respond to what is of God in everyone.

I feel sick, sometimes, at the thought of losing my life. Sometimes I fail myself on the journey. I have to learn to love myself, in all my weaknesses, when my writing stops, when my life stops, when my self-esteem drops like a stone into a well. Sometimes I shed tears at my loss of physical vitality. When I was beautiful, why did I not just go out there and love it? My spirit is more vital. As Bríd says: 'Enjoy your life.' As Mary T. says: 'Define expert!'

There are none.

For me this is still the challenge: to rise above my feelings of being unlovable; to rise above my relentless self-questioning and reach the cloud of acceptance. This is where the angel journey took me, to the first promise of that reaching.

I have written a book for other humans. Not intellectuals. Not theologians. Not visionaries. I'm writing; my soul is a writing soul. That's the main thing. I wondered when I would ever get back to it. All the rest is bullshit. I am writing about my frailties and my findings. But I'm a shadow.

A friend tells me, when I say this, 'You're a shadow of the light, Suzanne.' This is where the angel journeyers and I return in our rule of engagement. We bring lack to our conversations and we top up the dreaming self. Much as the story people, the story monks of our old days did. They are angels because they have a message for the new times.

I see myself alone on the hill, in the time I spent under the guidance of Dame Marie Herbert, naming myself after Vision Quest, only weeks away from losing everything I thought I had found again. Only weeks away from putting my bare feet on the right life path. The path of stones and uncertainties, magic and mundane, the path of goodbye to familiarity and embracing strangers in strange times. The name I chose on that occasion was Leanbh an tSolais, Child of the Light.

At that time, in Scotland, I danced with my shadow on a mountain-top and wanted never to come down. It was an exhilaration in a exhilarating year. The year of meeting the light in me, the year of relinquishing old love through new instincts, through messages coming from so deep within me, or without, or one and the same, that I had to be bedridden to stay still enough to get them. All the messages of my inner voice at that time were luminous.

I had the first spiritual rush that St Teresa of Avila, mystic contemporary and confidante of John of the Cross, identifies in her book *The Interior Castle*. This book was her answer to the communication she sought, the need to talk to her God in her own inner voice, at a time when it was considered that weak-minded women who prayed in such a way might be led astray by unguided practice.

Teresa knew the guidance came from inner knowing rather than outer instruction. She saw that Christ dwelt at the very centre of the soul; therefore our inner voice is the angelic voice, the mediator between supreme being and human being. She decided this: 'Mental prayer in my opinion is nothing else than an intimate sharing between friends.'

Teresa did not enjoy restrictions to her faith. She had visions and these visions reinforced her belief. She did not deny them at a time of Inquisition, at a time when many visionaries were tortured. She believed ordinary humans had the capacity to have visions. Everyone is close to God. In the angel journeyers I hear her echo.

The Interior Castle also talks of the time the communication fell silent. Mine did after the first rush. This book has brought me to recognise that from 2006 to 2009 I believed in nothing and trusted no one. I thought the darkness was my lack but now I know it to be an angelic darkness, a time of purgation in the truest sense of that word. I was alone. No voice took the anguish away from me. I was writing but I didn't believe in a word I was writing. The only faith I had was in my children.

I don't know how I sank so low but an experience of true self-neglect, a moment where I saw myself as I had become, a moment that brought a desire for death close to me, that moment took me to the bottom and gave me the option of rising to the surface or remaining in my self-made grave. *Angel Journey* is part of the story of that rise. I am back treading water, on the surface of a vast sea called faith.

Start your conversation. Who knows who will answer? Angelic beings and their message invite us to love ourselves as we truly are. To know ourselves is to know more of God.

I feel a feather of that exhilaration now brush past my face: expecting to fly has brought me closer to the ground. I am marked with the peace of my failures. I am looking from failure up, from gutter to stars, from unknowing to the great unknown. What is in me is replicated in the late spring sky. I am finding new energy for love, to love.

Love took away all my practices, all the faith I stored and left me empty and turned over. Then it brought me new messages, stronger and deeper, and made me less afraid to tell you, the person reading, about them. And in telling you I tell myself. The woman I once was, who had hopes of becoming something, became nothing. She thought the illness had been her lesson and then she found the recovery after illness brought more than lessons: it brought annihilation on angel wings. It brought annunciation through the shared rooms and insights of people the length and breadth of this small country with such a vast past and such a deep soul practice. Outside ritual, outside masses I stood at the back of for the lack of spirit in them, outside hierarchy, stands my unknown, waiting patiently for me. My angel. The shadow that was born in me and grows in me still. The guardian. The inspirer. The persuader that stature is always better than status and failure always better than false victories in arenas I want no part of. I am a woman. I am a mother. I am a friend. I am a lover. All these parts of me are known. But the unknown; this is the angel in me.

The spiritual journey is about action and not outcome. There is no conclusion, other than to accept that there is no conclusion.

The spiritual messages come from a place that knows us better than we know ourselves; they are working with a higher reasoning power than ours, a power that knows us and loves us better than we can know ourselves, or indeed love ourselves, since we don't know all there is to love.

I have met so many people on this journey. They tell me the same thing. Just have faith. When you do the incredible happens. This is the truth of me. This is the truth of you.